WIN A WEEKEND BREAK IN YORKSHIRE AND A YEAR'S SUPPLY OF YORKSHIRE TEA

Answer the questions overleaf and you could win a luxury weekend break in Harrogate for two people, with afternoon tea at Bettys Café Tea Rooms – and a year's supply of Yorkshire Tea.

Four runners-up will win a hamper from Bettys & Taylors of Harrogate.

While you're enjoying afternoon tea in one of the tea rooms in this book, why not have a go at our 'Teatime Quiz'? One lucky winner and their guest will enjoy a weekend break in Harrogate with afternoon tea at Bettys Café Tea Rooms, and they will also get to take home a year's supply of Yorkshire Tea. Four runners-up will receive a hamper from Bettys & Taylors of Harrogate. Just answer the questions below to be in with a chance of winning. You'll find some of the answers in this book.

Anna, Duchess of Bedford, is popularly credited with introducing the idea of afternoon tea. Suffering from hunger pains in the long gap between lunch and dinner, she ordered her maid to bring her tea and cakes each afternoon to alleviate these "sinking feelings". In which century did this happen?
a) 18th century   b) 20th century   c) 19th century

Which family tea merchant, founded by Charles Taylor in 1886, blends Yorkshire Tea?
a) Taylors of Harrogate   b) Taylors of Yorkshire   c) Taylors Tea

Bettys Café Tea Rooms is regarded as a quintessential English tea room, but it was actually founded by a Swiss Confectioner called Frederick Belmont in 1919. Today there are five Bettys Café Tea Rooms, but in which Yorkshire town was the very first Bettys opened?
a) Harrogate   b) York   c) Beverley

Just send your answers on a postcard, along with your name and address to:
Teatime Quiz, Freepost HG137, Harrogate HG2 7BR

The closing date to win this fabulous prize is 31st October 2004.
Two runner-up winners of the prize hamper will be drawn after the closing date of 30th April 2005, and a further two after the closing date of 31st October 2005.

Britain's Best Afternoon Tea

Maps prepared by the Cartography Department of The Automobile Association. Maps © Automobile Association Developments Limited 2004.

Typeset by Keene Repro, Andover
Cover photographs: courtesy of the Tea Council and front cover left AA/Richard Ireland, back cover AA/ Michael Busselle.
Printed and bound by Graficas estella, S.A., Navarra, Spain
Editor: Jane Gregory
Writers: Julia Hynard, Denise Laing
Images pages 3, 5, 7, 15, 16, 17 & 19 courtesy of The Tea Council and text pages 8, 9, 10, 11, 16, 17, 18, 64, 77, 140, 155 courtesy of The Tea Guild and Jane Pettigrew

A CIP catalogue record for this book is available from the British Library

ISBN 0 7495 39771

Published by AA trading which is a trading name of Automobile Association Developments Limited, whose registered office is Millstream, Maidenhead Road, Windsor, Berkshire, SL4 5GD

Registered number 1878835

A01837

CONTENTS

How to use the guide

The guide is divided into countries: England, Scotland, and Wales.

Each country is listed in county order, and then in approximate alphabetical town/village location within each county.

There is a county map on page 23 to help you locate counties within Britain. In the England section, counties are indicated at the top left or right side of each page.

Finding the Town
If you know which town you are looking for, refer to the index at the back of the guide. Towns are listed alphabetically, with their county, page number and

establishments in or closest to the town, or village, establishments are listed approximately alphabetically.

The tea shops and tea rooms in the guide with this symbol in their entry are all members of the The Tea Guild and have been inspected and approved by The Tea Council's inspectors.

AA Stars and Rosettes
The hotels in this guide have been inspected by the AA under the nationally recognised Star classification schemes, agreed between the AA, VisitBritain and the RAC, and enabling you to make your choice with confidence. Rosettes are awarded by the AA for food.

For a full explanation of these ratings and awards please see pages 14 & 15

The Example Tea Room
Genuine warm hospitality coupled with home from home comforts

❶ — ☎ 01234 567899 ⓕ 01234 567898
ⓔ e-mail@address.uk
ⓦ www.lovely.com
❷ — Map ref 6 - TQ40
❸ — LANCASTER, LA6 1XX
2m off B6254 Carnforth - Kirkby Lonsdale.
❹ — ☕ Open 10am-4pm; Tea served all day
Closed Sun, 25 Dec; Set tea price(s)
£5.50 - £10; Seats 45; No credit cards;
No Smoking; No Dogs; Parking 12

❺ — *T*his charming building dates in part from the 18th century. The conservatory, where tea is served, is an impressive Victorian structure, with palms and a fountain. Afternoon tea consists of a selection of finger sandwiches, freshly baked scones with clotted cream and preserves, tea bread and assorted pastries. Lady Anne's Tea goes further, with English muffins and gateaux.

RECOMMENDED IN THE AREA

Lancaster; Morecombe; Blackpool

1 *Contact Details*
Telephone and fax numbers, e-mail and website addresses are shown as provided by the establishments.
Please Note - Website Addresses These are included where they have been supplied by the establishment and lead you to websites that are not under the control of The Automobile Association Developments Ltd. The Automobile Association Developments Ltd has no control over and will not accept any responsibility or liability in respect of the material on any such website. By including the addresses of third party websites the AA does not intend to solicit business.

2 *Map Reference*
The map refers to the town or village. The map page number refers to the atlas at the front of the guide, and is followed by the two-figure National Grid Reference. To find the location, read the first figure horizontally and the second figure vertically within the lettered square. Maps locating each establishment can also be found on the AA website, www.theAA.com

3 *Address and Directions*
The full postal address of each establishment is given, followed by brief directions.

4 *Establishment Details*
Where the establishments have given us up-to-date information, the following details are included:
• Prices for set teas
• Number of seats
• Smoking restrictions
  (see below)
• Opening times, and times
  when tea is served
• Days or times of year when closed
• Whether dogs are allowed
• Whether parking is provided

5 *Description*
The description of the establishment includes information about the tea room or lounge and the type of food available.

6 *Recommended in the Area*
We asked the establishments to tell us about places to visit in their area which they recommend to their guests.

The AA Days Out Guide, available from bookshops or the AA website, may also prove useful in finding things to do in the area.

Local Specialities
At the start of each county in England, and also for Scotland and Wales, we have highlighted traditional tea time delicacies that you should look out for.

Hotel Listings
We have included a listing of hotels that offer afternoon tea at the end of the London, Scotland and Wales sections.

www.theAA.com
The AA website gives details of all AA recommended accommodation, including all the places to stay listed in this guide.

www.tea.co.uk
The Tea Council website gives details of all Tea Guild Members.

Complaints
Readers who have any cause to complain are urged to do so on the spot. This should provide an opportunity for the proprietor to correct matters. If a personal approach fails, readers should inform AA Hotel Services, Fanum House, Basingstoke RG21 4EA. The AA does not however undertake to obtain compensation for complaints.

Smoking Restrictions
Smoking restrictions for hotels are given for the tea lounge only and not for the establishment as a whole (unless otherwise stated). If smoking regulations are of importance to you please make sure that you check the exact details with the establishment when booking.

What is The Tea Council?

The Tea Council is a non-profit organisation representing the interests of the major tea producing countries and the UK tea packers. The Council acts as a spokesperson for the tea industry on a wide range of topics, and is also involved in promoting the health benefits of tea drinking.

One of its most important initiatives is The Tea Guild, an organisation that encourages the tradition of excellence in tea brewing, and reflects the importance of taking tea as an enjoyable social ritual.

The Tea Guild

The Tea Guild was founded in 1995, after an independent survey, commissioned by The Tea Council, found that out of the thousands of beverage serving outlets across the country, few were serving tea to the standards desired by The Tea Council.

The Guild was set up to provide recognition to those outlets meeting these high standards.

Membership of The Tea Guild is strictly by invitation only. When a tea room is interested in becoming a member, they are visited by an incognito tea taster. If that establishment complies with The Tea Council's high standards (see page 10) they are then invited to become a member.

Tea Guild members are able to benefit from the resources and reputation of The Tea Council , and from publicity and promotions organised by the Council.
They also receive automatic entry into the annual search for *Top Tea Place of the Year* or the *Top London Afternoon Tea Award* – both

competitions attract extensive coverage in the press.

What defines the ideal tea shop or tea room?

The ideal catering outlet that The Tea Council looks for to join The Guild must focus particularly on tea. They must serve good quality tea, offer a wide selection of tea to cater for all tastes and they must brew and serve these teas well. The outlet must also offer an atmosphere in which customers feel welcome, comfortable, relaxed, and are treated with care and courtesy.

This sort of outlet might be one of the following:

• a traditional tea shop or tea room in a country cottage

• a traditional tea shop in a town centre in, for example, a Georgian house or a Victorian shop

• a hotel lounge that serves morning coffee, lunchtime snacks, cocktails etc., and usually a set afternoon tea with sandwiches, scones and pastries

• a restaurant that doubles as a tea room during the afternoon and offers good teas throughout the day and after dinner

• a tea area attached to or part of an antiques market, garden centre, or craft and art gallery

• a modern tea bar, similar to a coffee bar but serving mainly tea, and which may offer take-away tea as well as pots of tea to drink in the shop

• an oriental-style noodle or dim sum restaurant that serves an excellent range of Chinese teas as well as other black, green and flavoured teas from around the world.

The Crockery and Teapots Used by Tea Shops

The teapots, cups and saucers, general crockery and cutlery chosen by individual tea places can vary enormously and should link with the overall style, theme and atmosphere of the venue. A top quality tea room may offer different brewing and drinking vessels according to the types of tea they serve.

Teapots

Pots made from certain materials are not suitable for the successful brewing of tea. These are aluminium, pewter, enamel, uncoated iron and plastic. They may taint the tea or emit undesirable substances into the infusion.

The best teapots are made from porcelain, bone china, glazed stoneware, unglazed Chinese red earthenware, silver and glass. These lose heat slowly from the outside and maintain a good temperature inside. When the visual effect of the brewing of the leaves and the colour of the liquor is required, glass is excellent. The size and shape of the teapot is very important. It is essential that the correct amount of tea and water are used in each pot and that the leaves have enough room to move around in order to absorb water and release their colour and flavour into the water.

Cups and Saucers

There is no doubt that porcelain and bone china make the best teacups. They keep the tea hot, they are more elegant and they are easy to lift.

But depending on the style and theme of a teashop, different materials may be used. However, the heavy stoneware and pottery often used for catering tablewares allow the tea to cool more quickly than porcelain and bone china and are generally less acceptable to most people.

The shape of cups is also important. A wide top allows the tea to cool faster while taller, narrower shapes are excellent for piping the aroma of the tea. This is important with some of the fine China green and oolong teas.

Cups, mugs or bowls?

For traditional British tea drinking, cups and saucers are best. For oriental teas (oolongs and green teas from China and Japan) little bowls or tall straight-sided cups with no handles are culturally correct and add an interesting and colourful element to the tea drinking experience.

The Tea Council's Awards

The Tea Council rates establishments who are members of The Tea Guild by matching their performance against strict criteria. A summary of these is given below.

Tea shops, tea rooms and tea lounges in London hotels are awarded a number of 'teacup' symbols from one to five, depending on how well the judges consider they have upheld the high standards of The Guild and the tradition of tea.

Hygiene and Décor

Cleanliness and décor are obviously very important. In addition to The Tea Council's exacting standards of hygiene, there should be no dust, stains on teacloths, or anything that might be distasteful to a paying customer. Any food preparation areas in view must be clean, with raw and cooked foods kept separately.

Crockery

Tea should be served in a pot, with enough tea/tea bags to ensure an appropriate strength of brew. All pottery or china must be in good condition with no cracks, chips or stains. Stainless-steel milk and water jugs are not favoured. If loose-leaf tea is served, a strainer or infuser should always accompany it. There should be a different strainer for each type of tea (so that one type is not being strained through another).

Staff Attitude and Efficiency

Staff should be friendly and well
g a reasonable
different varieties of
service should be
tive.

Variety of Tea

Different varieties of tea should be listed on the menu. There should be a good range of teas from the main growing countries, and both leaf and bag tea should be on offer.

Staff Knowledge of Tea

Staff should know the difference between the teas available and be able advise customers depending on their tastes, and also give advice about whether the tea chosen should be taken with milk or lemon.

Milk

To cater for all tastes and diets, full fat semi-skimmed and skimmed milk should be available, with semi-skimmed milk being offered as the norm. A slice of lemon should also be available if required.

Sugar

Lumped sugar is best – in a covered sugar bowl if possible. Tongs should be provided where sugar lumps are served. Sweeteners should also be available.

Cakes and Foods

Fresh, tasty home-baked foods are looked for, a wide selection on offer, served attractively and stored hygienically.

Overall Ambience and Value for Money

Afternoon tea should be treated as an 'experience'; therefore customers should be offered a relaxing, interesting and enjoyable environment in which to enjoy it.

Award Winners 2004

Top Tea Place Winner

Bird on the Rock Tea Room, Clungunford, Shropshire

This delightfully atmospheric tea room achieved high marks in all categories judged, and excellent customer care was displayed by the friendly staff. Douglas and Annabel Hawkes provide an excellent selection of delicious home-made food, and serve a wide range of the best quality tea to their customers. Teas, jams, chutneys, cards and games are available for purchase.

Runner Up

Cemlyn Restaurant and Tea Shop, Harlech, Gwynedd

This friendly establishment has scored consistently high marks all year. The owner's warm welcome and the staff's friendliness and efficiency were judged to be of the highest standard. The variety and quality of the home-made food sampled was excellent and extremely good value, and a substantial list of different teas was available. The owner's knowledge of teas and keenness to advise was also praised.

Awards of Excellence – forty of the tea shops and tea rooms in the guide have been chosen to receive the annual Tea Guild Award of Excellence. Look out for mention of this in their entries.

Top Country House Hotel Winner

Cliveden, Taplow, Buckinghamshire

A new award, and a well deserved win for this wonderfully, historic country mansion. Cliveden's elegant but relaxed atmosphere makes afternoon tea here a very enjoyable experience.

The décor is immaculate with beautiful antique furniture, paintings and wonderful floral arrangements. Staff are helpful and welcoming, and offer a choice of rooms in which to take tea. Orders are taken and served promptly, the afternoon tea is excellent and there are a good variety of teas on offer. Those sampled were of a very good flavour and served at the correct temperature.

Award of Excellence

Llangoed Hall Hotel, Brecon, Powys

Top London Afternoon Tea Award Winner

The Ritz

Despite fierce competition The Ritz was considered to be the most impressive venue for tea in London. The maximum number of marks were achieved in most areas. The friendly, helpful and welcoming staff really help to make the experience memorable. The cakes and sandwiches offered are delicious, and beautifully presented with different types of bread used for each sandwich. The selection of teas tasted were served perfectly and with helpful advice from the waiters. All were of an excellent quality and flavour, well brewed and with a lovely colour, and most importantly, offered 'piping hot'.

Bird on the Rock Tea Room

Cemlyn Restaurant and Tea Shop

Cliveden

The Ritz

A LOVELY CUP OF TEA

Whilst this book is packed full of wonderful places to take afternoon tea, every day tea drinkers all over the country discover the secret of enjoying a lovely cup of tea at home... Yorkshire Tea, a rich full-flavoured blend, the likes of which you might not have tasted for years.

Yorkshire Tea is blended by one of the country's few remaining family tea merchants, Taylors of Harrogate. The business was founded in 1886 by an energetic Yorkshireman, Charles Taylor. Charles set about testing water across Yorkshire so that he could blend the perfect tea for every village and town. The local grocers that Charles supplied were delighted with these blends, encouraging him to open his own chain of tea rooms –

Charles Taylor.

the Kiosks, and the very grand Café Imperial in Harrogate – a rendezvous for smart and discerning ladies with a passion for afternoon tea. By the 1920s, Harrogate had a reputation as one of the most fashionable spa towns in England and boasted over a dozen of the country's leading cafés, all serving Charles Taylor's tea. After Charles's death, his business joined forces with one of these cafés, another family business called Bettys.

The original Café Imperial in Harrogate.

Taking tea at Bettys.

Today, the third generation of Tea Buyers at Taylors of Harrogate upholds the time-honoured traditions established by Charles Taylor. Indeed, the way the Tea Buyers select teas for their Yorkshire Tea blend would be very familiar to Charles Taylor. Every single tea they buy is tasted – often over 300 teas a day – to ensure it meets the grade. Only those that give the perfect balance of strength, colour, flavour, and character are selected. And Yorkshire Tea is still blended to suit the water, so you can enjoy a proper cup of tea… no matter where you live.

TEATIME TREATS

What better accompaniment to a cup of tea than a handmade cake, or perhaps a biscuit or two to dunk! The Yorkshire Tea Loaf and Yorkshire Tea Biscuits are made by hand, to traditional recipes, at Bettys Craft Bakery in Harrogate. The Tea Loaf is deliciously moist and packed full of vine fruits, whole natural cherries, and spices. But what makes it really special is the fact that the fruit is soaked overnight in Yorkshire Tea. The luxury shortbread biscuits are rich and buttery with a hint of spice and, just like the Tea Loaf, contain that special ingredient – a rich infusion of Yorkshire Tea.

You'll find the Yorkshire Tea Loaf and Yorkshire Tea Biscuits in selected Sainsburys, Morrisons, Co-op, and Safeway supermarkets.

Bettys Master Baker Paul Gray, with a batch of freshly baked Tea Loaves.

Afternoon tea at home.

AA Classifications and Awards

The AA inspects and classifies hotels, guest houses and restaurants with rooms. Establishments applying for AA quality assessment are visited on a 'mystery guest' basis by one of the AA's team of qualified accommodation inspectors. Inspectors stay overnight to make a thorough test of the accommodation, food and hospitality offered. On settling the bill the following morning they identify themselves and ask to be shown round the premises. The inspector completes a full report, making a recommendation for the appropriate level of quality (see below). The establishments in this guide have been recommended by AA inspectors for their excellent hospitality, accommodation and food.

AA Star Classification

If you stay in a one-star hotel you should expect a relatively informal yet competent style of service and an adequate range of facilities, including a television in the lounge or bedroom and a reasonable choice of hot and cold dishes. The majority of bedrooms are en suite

with a bath or shower room always available.

A two-star hotel is run by smartly and professionally presented management and offers at least one restaurant or dining room for breakfast and dinner, while a three-star hotel includes direct dial telephones, a wide selection of drinks in the bar and last orders for dinner no earlier than 8pm.

A four-star hotel is characterised by uniformed, well-trained staff with additional services, a night porter and a serious approach to cuisine. Finally, and most luxurious of all, is the five-star hotel offering many extra facilities, attentive staff, top quality rooms and a full concierge service. A wide selection of drinks, including cocktails, is available in the bar, and the impressive menu reflects and complements the hotel's own style of cooking. The AA's Top 200 Hotels in Britain and Ireland are identified by red stars. These stand out as the very best and range from large luxury destination hotels to snug country inns. To find further details see the AA's web site at www.theAA.com

AA Rosette Awards

Out of around 40,000 UK restaurants, the AA awards rosettes to around 1,800. The following is an outline of what to expect from restaurants with AA Rosette Awards.

🏵 Excellent local restaurants serving food prepared with care, understanding and skill, using good quality ingredients. These are restaurants that stand out in their local area. The same expectations apply to hotel restaurants where guests should be able to eat with confidence and a sense of anticipation. Around 50% of AA-inspected restaurants have one Rosette.

🏵 🏵 The best local restaurants, which aim for and achieve higher standards, better consistency and where a greater precision is apparent in the cooking. There will be obvious attention to the selection of quality ingredients. Around 40% of AA-inspected restaurants have two Rosettes.

🏵 🏵 🏵 Outstanding restaurants that demand recognition well beyond their local area. The cooking will be underpinned by the selection and sympathetic treatment of the highest quality ingredients. Timing, seasoning and the judgement of flavour combinations will be consistently excellent, supported by other elements such as intelligent service and a well-chosen wine list. Around 150 restaurants have three Rosettes.

🏵 🏵 🏵 🏵 Amongst the very best restaurants in the British Isles where the cooking demands national recognition. These restaurants will exhibit intense ambition, a passion for excellence, superb technical skills and remarkable consistency. They will combine appreciation of culinary traditions with a passionate desire for further exploration and improvement. Around a dozen restaurants have four Rosettes.

🏵 🏵 🏵 🏵 🏵 The finest restaurants in the British Isles, where the cooking stands comparison with the best in the world. These restaurants will have highly individual voices, exhibit breathtaking culinary skills and set the standards to which others aspire. Around half a dozen restaurants have five Rosettes.

The Tradition of Tea

Over 40% of what we drink daily in Britain – apart from tap water – is tea, which makes it the nation's favourite drink. At times of crisis our first resort is the kettle, for there's nothing like the comfort of a freshly brewed cuppa. We've been supping the stuff for over 300 years and drink an average of three cups a day. Whatever the occasion, wedding or wake, everything stops for tea and the inevitable gathering around the steaming pot. Tea is not, however, native to the British soil, so how did this love affair begin?

Chinese Roots

Legend has it that tea drinking began in China more than 5,000 years ago, when Emperor Shen Nung, a man of serious scientific principles, decreed that all drinking water should be boiled for reasons of hygiene. One day, while travelling far from home, the court stopped to boil up some water, dried leaves from a bush fell into the pot and the inevitable occurred. Tea-drinking spread throughout Chinese society, and in 800 AD the first book about tea was written by a man called Lu Yu, brought up as an orphaned child by Buddhist monks. Through many years of observation he recorded methods of tea cultivation and preparation, which led to the creation of a tea service, informed by his Zen Buddhist approach, which was carried by Buddhist priests to imperial Japan.

The 'Father of Tea' in Japan was Yeisei, a Buddhist priest who brought tea seeds into the country from China. He believed that tea was an aid to religious meditation, and in Japan the association between tea and Zen Buddhism remains. The service of tea was elevated to a high art in Japanese society, inspiring a complex and stylised ritual and even its own form of architecture.

The European Experience

A Portuguese Jesuit, Father Jasper de Cruz, was the first European to write about tea with any real authority in 1560. He was a missionary on the Portuguese navy's first trading trip with China when he encountered the exotic beverage. Prior to this, earlier European travellers had been uncertain as to what tea was actually for, and seemed under some misapprehension that it should be boiled and eaten as a vegetable. Holland at this time had close affiliations with Portugal and also entered into the tea trade.

When tea first arrived in Europe in 1610, its immense cost made it the preserve of the wealthy, but as its popularity grew, the price fell and it was swept up in the prevailing passion for all things Oriental. The first mention of milk being added to the brew was observed by the Marquise de Seven in 1680, though the popularity of tea in France was relatively short lived. Tea came to Russia in 1618, as a gift from the Emperor of China to the Tsar. The Russians developed a taste for the stuff, but they traded overland by camel – tea for furs – over a long and perilous route.

Tea In Britain & The Colonies

Britain was the last of the three great seafaring nations to join the Chinese and East Indian trade routes. Under a charter granted by Elizabeth I, East India Company ships reached China in 1637, but it was not until 1644 that any tea dealing was recorded. Sailors returning from the Far East introduced tea to the London coffee houses and by 1700 there were

more than 500 such establishments serving the drink.

King Charles II grew up in exile in France and Holland, returning to re-establish the monarchy in 1660. He married the Portuguese Infanta Catherine de Braganza in 1662, and both were confirmed tea drinkers. Catherine brought chests of tea from Portugal as part of her dowry and the royal couple established the tea habit in Britain as a social and family ritual.

During the 18th century, tea drinking spread to wealthy American colonists. Anger over the high taxes England levied on tea turned to protest with the Boston Tea Party in 1773, an event that triggered the American colonies' fight for independence.

When tea was first taken up in the grander British homes, it was served at the end of the evening's entertainment, before the ladies went to bed. From the 1730s, London's pleasure gardens at Vauxhall and Ranelagh began serving tea, to round off an evening of dancing and fireworks, and soon tea gardens were a popular phenomenon all over the country.

The British Tradition

The tradition of afternoon tea is credited to Anna, Duchess of Bedford, who in the early 1800s had the idea of serving tea with a little something to eat to stave off the pangs between lunch and dinner. This quickly became the custom in polite society, and an enjoyable occasion for friends and family to get together.

Tea did not become widely available to working people until the mid to late 19th century, with the importation of cheaper tea grown in India and Sri Lanka and the advent of the clipper ships, which speeded up transportation. The burgeoning temperance movement also necessitated a cheap alternative to the usual beer or ale. For labourers, a cup of tea meant a break from work, the reviving comfort of a hot drink and the stimulus of the caffeine content. The high tea of the ordinary folk was different from the afternoon tea of high society. It was the main meal of the day for those who could not afford a proper cooked meal, comprising bread, meats, cakes or pastries, served with a good strong cuppa.

The country's first tea shop was started in 1864 by the manageress of the Aerated Bread Company, when the company directors permitted her to serve refreshments to favoured customers. Demand for the service grew, sparking a trend for similar establishments across Great Britain. These did much to liberate the lives of women, as it was considered perfectly proper for a woman to meet friends in a tea shop without the imposition of a chaperone. Today, with our Guide, we honour this unnamed woman as the founder of a fine tradition proudly upheld by a grateful nation.

What is Tea?

The making and drinking of tea is a deeply imbedded national tradition and many of us would struggle through the day without its comforting, thirst-quenching and reviving properties, yet how much do we know about this exotic plant from faraway lands?

All the tea drunk in the world is made from the leaves of the same evergreen, tropical plant, a member of the Camellia family *(Camellia sinensis)*, which has shiny green pointed leaves and was originally indigenous to both China and India.

In its wild condition, tea will grow into a tree some 30 metres high, but under cultivation the plant is kept at around a metre for ease of picking. The bush is trained to grow into a fan shape, with a flat top called a plucking table, and it takes between three and five years to reach maturity. Only the top two leaves and a bud are picked from the sprigs on the plucking table, and the rate of re-growth will depend on the altitude at which the bush is grown. A tea bush at sea level will replace itself more quickly than a bush grown at a higher level where the air will be cooler. The bushes are picked, generally by hand, every 7-14 days.

A skilled tea 'plucker' can pick up to 35 kilograms in a day, which will produce 7.5-9 kilograms of processed black tea. Most factories produce black tea, where the leaf is dried, broken, fermented and dried or fired again. For green tea, the withered leaf is steamed and rolled before drying, to stop the veins in the leaf from breaking, thus preventing oxidisation or fermentation.

Tea grows best in a warm, humid climate where there is at least 100 centimetres of rain a year. It likes a deep, light, acidic and well-drained soil. Appropriate conditions might be found at sea level or up to 2,100 metres above sea level. The flavour of the tea will depend on the type of soil the plant is grown in, the altitude and the climate. The processing of the leaf and the blending of leaves from various places will also affect the character of the final product.

There are more than 1,500 teas to choose from, and tea is grown in around 30 different countries around the world, including:

China

For centuries China tea was the only tea known to the Western world and was extensively used in blends. China remains a major tea producer, but is best known now for speciality teas such as Lapsang Souchong, Keemun, the Oolongs and green teas.

India

The tea plant is indigenous to the Assam area of India, but the first tea grown commercially in the country was brought as seeds and cuttings from China. In 1835 The East India Company established experimental tea plantations in Assam, and by the 1840s Indian tea was being exported to England on a regular basis. Tea picking in Assam and Darjeeling is seasonal, and Darjeeling is known as the Champagne of teas. Nilgiri, grown high in the hills, is not dissimilar to the teas of Sri Lanka.

Indonesia

The Dutch East India Company began the tea trade in these Southeast Asian islands around 200 years ago, and tea from Indonesia, India and Ceylon dominated the market for black tea until World War II. The industry did pick up after the war, and these days the light, fragrant Indonesian teas are largely used for blending.

Kenya

Kenya is a very fertile country, with a climate that allows tea to be picked all year round. Tea production in Kenya is believed to date from 1903 when two acres of tea was planted using imported seeds from India. Today Kenyan is the largest exporter of black tea in the world, and over 50% of tea imported into the UK is from Kenya.

Malawi

The first African country to experiment with tea planting, Malawi has been trading tea since the 1870s, and was also the first African country to adopt the cloning or cuttings method to refurbish tea plantations. Though it may not be as well known as the speciality names, Malawian tea is featured in many well-known British blends. Like other East African teas, the product is bright and colourful with a reddish tint.

Sri Lanka

Sri Lanka, formerly known as Ceylon, was well known for its coffee in the 19th century, but in the 1870s the Ceylon coffee crops were decimated by coffee rust fungus. Many planters followed the example of Scotsman James Taylor who had successfully planted the island's first tea estate in the hills above Kandy. Sri Lanka produces high, medium and low-grown teas, each with its own character.

Tanzania

Tea production really took off between the wars under the British flag. The country produces high, medium and low-grown tea, each with its own characteristics, but still discernibly East African.

Zimbabwe

Tea was originally grown under the influence of the British. The first irrigated tea estate was established here, a necessity in Zimbabwe, as the low annual rainfall is only about half that usually required for tea production.

Useful Information

Fire Precautions and Safety

Many of the hotels listed in the guide are subject to the requirements of the Fire Precautions Act of 1971, and should display details of how to summon assistance in the event of an emergency at night.

Codes of Practice

The AA encourages the use of The Hotel Industry Voluntary Code of Booking Practice in appropriate establishments. Its prime objective is to ensure that the customer is clear about the price and the exact services and facilities being purchased, before entering into a contractually binding agreement. If the price has not been previously confirmed in writing, the guest should be handed a card at the time of registration, stipulating the total obligatory charge.

The Tourism (Sleeping Accommodation Price Display) Order 1977 compels hotels, motels, guest houses, farmhouses, inns and self-catering accommodation with four or more letting bedrooms to display in entrance halls the minimum and maximum prices charged for each category of room. This order complements the Voluntary Code of Booking Practice.

Dogs

Establishments which do not normally accept dogs may accept guide dogs. Some establishments that accept dogs may restrict the size and breed of dogs permitted and the rooms into which they may be taken. Please check the conditions when booking.

Children

Restrictions for children may be mentioned in the description. Some hotels may offer free accommodation to children when they share their parents' room. Please note that this information may be subject to change without notice and it is essential to check when booking.

London Congestion Charging Scheme

From 17 Feb 2003 Transport for London introduced a congestion charging scheme for most vehicles being used in a designated zone in Central London (roughly all the roads inside the Inner Ring Road).

The charge is an area licence – vehicles used in the central London area must be registered. Drivers pay £5 for the day (the zone operates 7am-6.30pm weekdays) and can cross into and out of the zone as often as they wish within the day. If your journey takes you into the charging zone you must either pre-pay the £5 charge or pay it before 10pm that day. Between 10pm and midnight the charge increases to £10 to encourage prompt payment. The system is controlled using a database of registered car registration numbers and a network of numberplate-reading cameras. At midnight each day all paid accounts are deleted from the system. Any vehicle recorded as having been in the zone during charging hours but with an unpaid account must pay a penalty charge. Payment can be made at any time, via the call centre – 0845 900 1234; via the congestion charging website *www.cclondon.com* or at paystations, selected petrol stations and retailers displaying the PayPoint logo.

For further details on London Congestion Charges see the AA website *www.TheAA.com*. The AA produces a Central Congestion Charging Zone Map obtainable from bookshops or from the AA Travel Bookshop on 01256 491524.

County Index

The county map shown here will help you identify the counties within each country. The England section of the guide has the county names in the panel at the edge of each page. To find towns featured in the guide use the map pages which follow, and the index at the back of the book. The numbers below refer to the numbers on the map.

England

1   Bedfordshire
2   Berkshire
3   Bristol
4   Buckinghamshire
5   Cambridgeshire
6   Greater Manchester
7   Herefordshire
8   Hertfordshire
9   Leicestershire
10   Northamptonshire
11   Nottinghamshire
12   Rutland
13   Staffordshire
14   Warwickshire
15   West Midlands
16   Worcestershire

Scotland

17   City of Glasgow
18   Clackmannanshire
19   East Ayrshire
20   East Dunbartonshire
21   East Renfrewshire
22   Perth & Kinross
23   Renfrewshire
24   South Lanarkshire
25   West Dunbartonshire

Wales

26   Blaenau Gwent
27   Bridgend
28   Caerphilly
29   Denbighshire
30   Flintshire
31   Merthyr Tydfil
32   Monmouthshire
33   Neath Port Talbot
34   Newport
35   Rhondda Cynon Taff
36   Torfaen
37   Vale of Glamorgan
38   Wrexham

C ounty & Country Index

KEY TO ATLAS PAGES

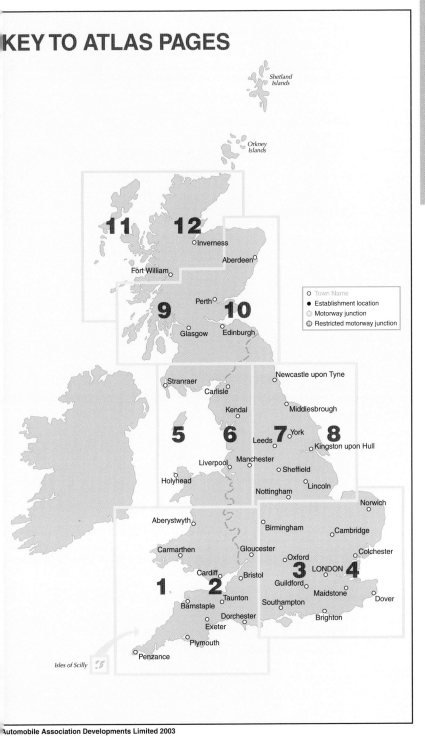

Shetland Islands

Orkney Islands

11 12

Inverness

Aberdeen

Fort William

O	Town Name
●	Establishment location
Ⓜ	Motorway junction
⓶	Restricted motorway junction

Perth 10

9

Glasgow Edinburgh

Stranraer

Newcastle upon Tyne

Carlisle

Kendal Middlesbrough

5 6 7 York 8

Leeds

Liverpool Manchester

Holyhead Sheffield

Kingston upon Hull

Nottingham Lincoln

Aberystwyth Norwich

Birmingham Cambridge

Carmarthen Gloucester Colchester

Cardiff Oxford

1 2 Bristol 3 LONDON 4

Guildford

Barnstaple Taunton Southampton Maidstone Dover

Dorchester Brighton

Exeter

Plymouth

Isles of Scilly Penzance

Automobile Association Developments Limited 2003

23

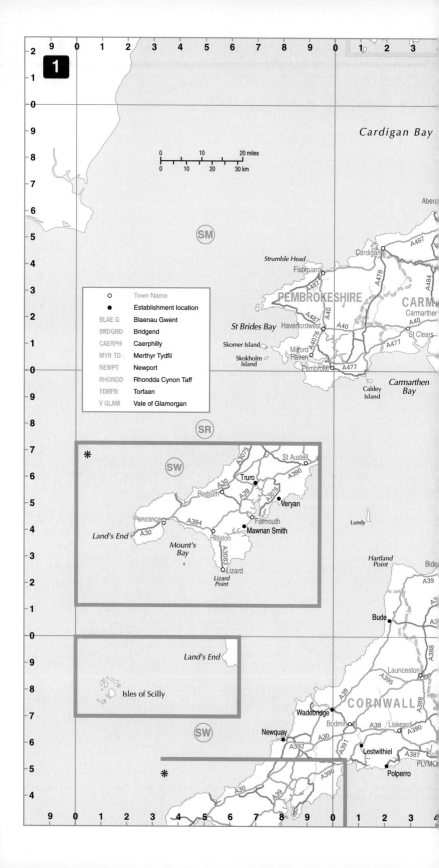

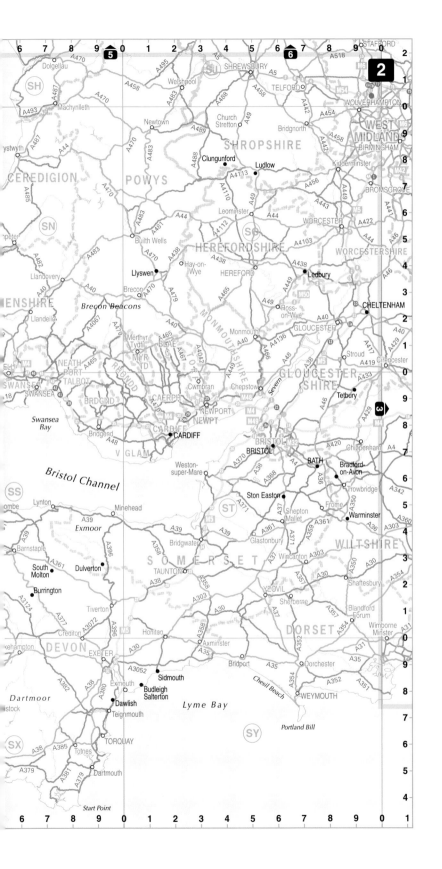

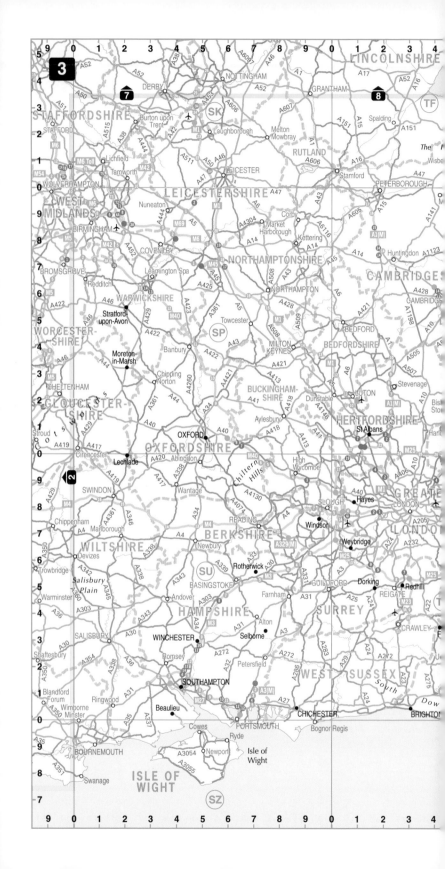

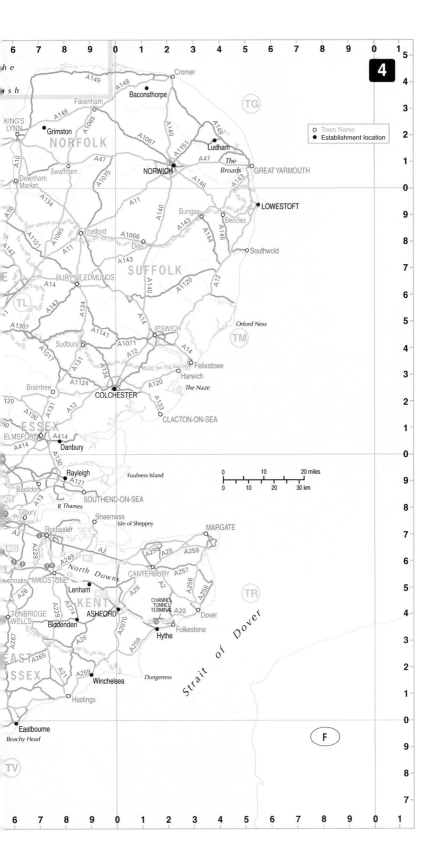

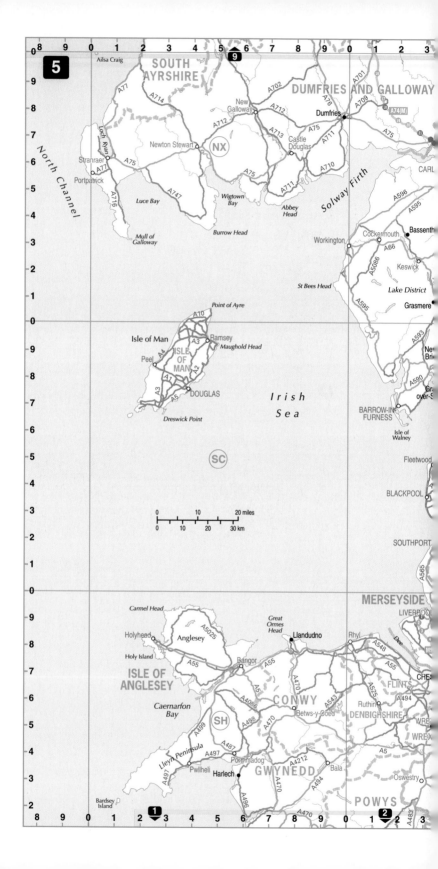

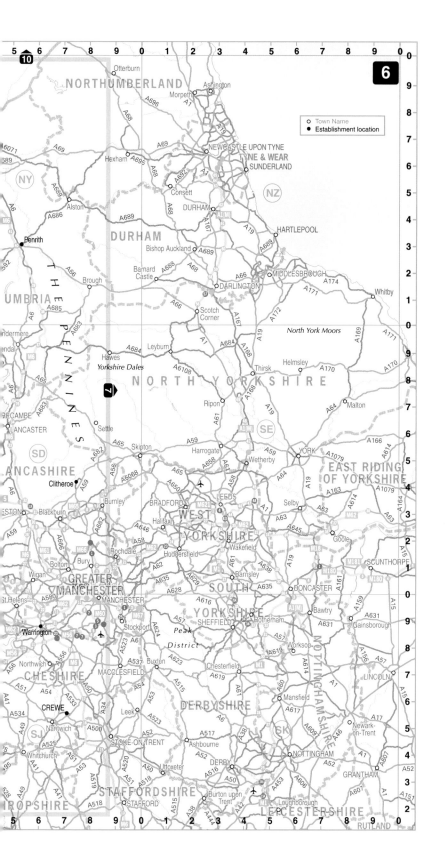

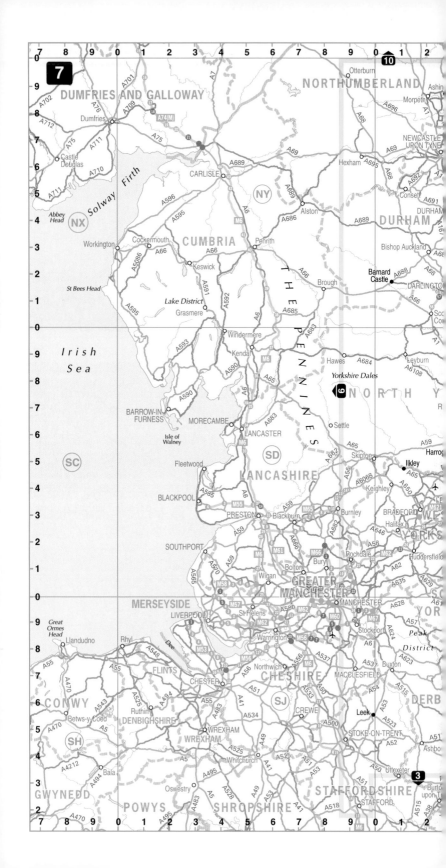

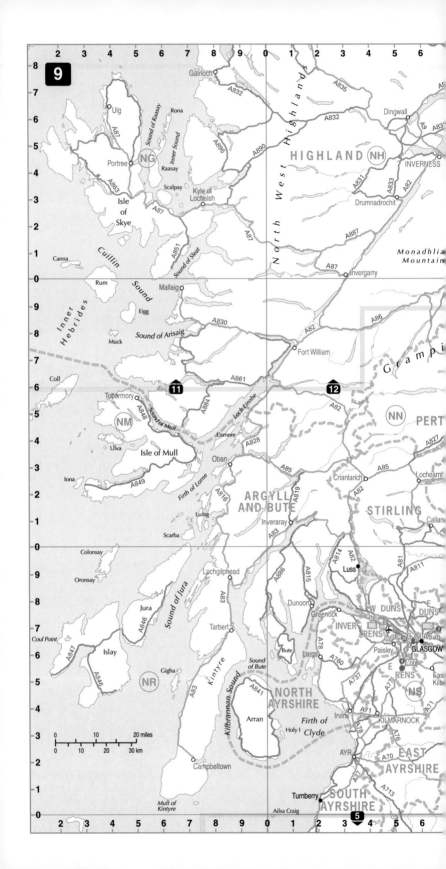

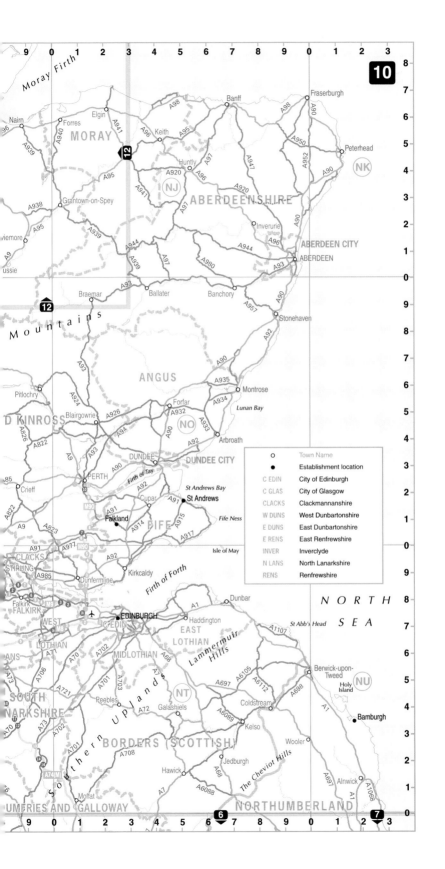

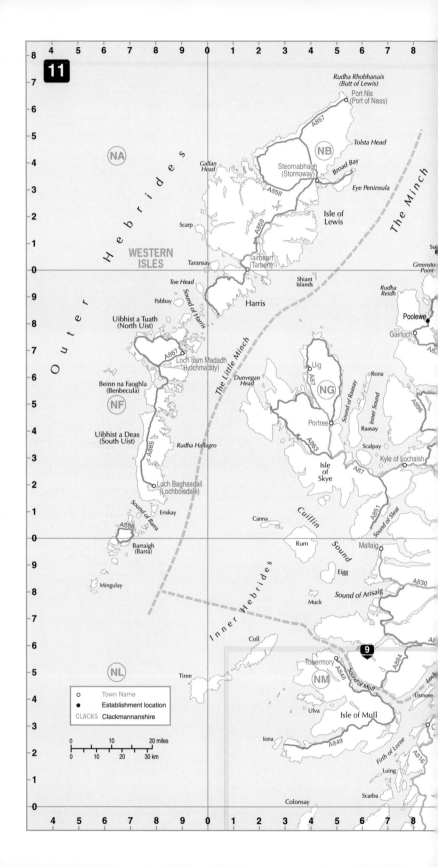

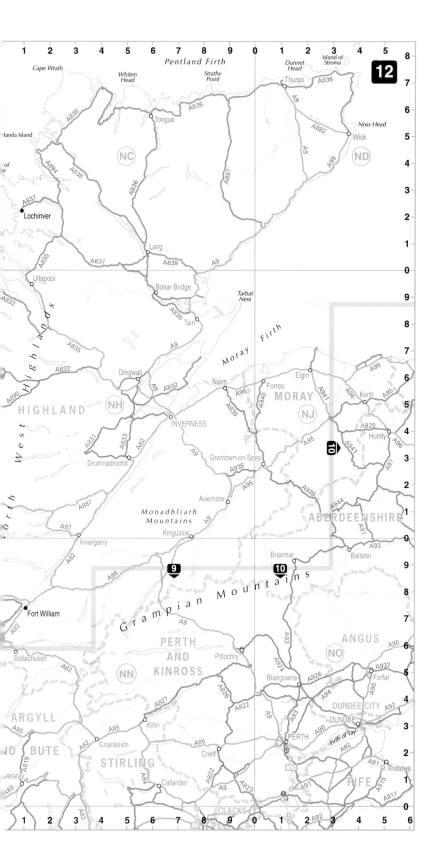

Berkshire

Apples and cherries have traditionally been grown in Berkshire and incorporated into delicious pies, tarts and turnovers. More frugal, yet nonetheless tasty fare, is 'Poor Knights of Windsor', a dish of stale bread dipped in a mixture of egg, milk and wine, fried and served with sugar and jam, or cinnamon. (The original Poor Knights of Windsor date back to the 14th century, and were a military order set up by King Edward III).

Another filling local delicacy is bacon pudding, a boiled pudding made from suet pastry with onions and fat bacon, guaranteed to keep you going until teatime.

*T*he Crooked House of Windsor Café-Tea Room

Historic building renowned for its eccentric tilt

☎ 01753 857534
✉ manager@
   crooked-house.com
ⓦ www.crooked-house.com

Map ref 4 - SU97

51 High Street, WINDSOR, SL4 1LR
☕ Open 9am-6pm; Tea served all day; Closed 25-26 Dec; Booking possible; Seats 38 + 12 outside; No Smoking

*T*his fine old property developed its characteristic crookedness after being restructured in 1718 with unseasoned green oak. A secret passageway running from the basement to Windsor Castle, now blocked, was reputedly used for illicit trysts between King Charles II and his mistress Nell Gwynne. The tea rooms occupy two floors, with views of the Changing of the Guard from upstairs.

Morning goods, light lunches, classic British dishes, Victorian-style afternoon teas and high teas are served, and a new development for April 2004 is baking on the premises, an extended pre-theatre opening. Teas, books, artworks an baked goods are available to buy. Small dogs permitted well controlled.

RECOMMENDED IN THE AREA
Windsor Castle; Savill Garden; Frogmore House

Bristol

Sugar to sweeten our teatime specialities has long been associated with the City of Bristol. The importation of sugar from the Caribbean during the era of the iniquitous slave trade, from 1698, laid the foundation for a major sugar processing industry in the city.

Bristol is also home to a renowned cream sherry, bottled in 'Bristol blue', the flagship product of Harveys, a company established in 1796. The great English classic, sherry trifle, is believed to date from the late 16th century, beginning as a simple syllabub-type concoction and developing over the years to its many-layered complexity of sherry-soaked sponge, fruit, custard and cream.

*B*ristol Marriott Royal Hotel ★★★★ ◉◉

Home-made pastries served in a luxurious hotel drawing room

🕿 0117 925 5100
🖷 0117 925 1515
🖃 bristol.royal@marriotthotels.co.uk
🌐 www.go.marriott.com/brsry

Map ref 2 - ST67

College Green, BRISTOL, BS1 5TA
Next to cathedral.
☕ Tea served 2pm-6pm daily; tea price(s) from £8.95; Seats 50; Air con; Dogs allowed on request; Parking 200 (charged)
🛏 242 Rooms; S from £75, D from £110

*S*plendid Victorian surroundings blend with stylish modern luxury to create an ideal setting for afternoon tea at this superb hotel. Easy to find, it stands next to the cathedral in the city centre; once inside, the positive first impressions are heightened by polished mahogany and marble, and bright chandeliers. Tea is served amid lavish comfort in the Club Lounge and the Drawing Room, and there are also tables outside for warm afternoons. Home-made pastries and cakes created by the award-winning kitchen's speciality chef are served at tea time, and those seeking a more filling meal will find a choice of sandwiches and wraps.

RECOMMENDED IN THE AREA
Bristol Hippodrome; Bristol Old Vic;
SS Great Britain

Buckinghamshire

Buckinghamshire is known for its rich and fertile farmland, and was once one of London's main suppliers of milk. Famously home to the Aylesbury duck, long believed to be the most delicious in Britain (although many birds referred to as such these days are cross breeds), Buckinghamshire was also once well known for plums, grown to make prunes, and also to provide dye for the Luton hat factory. Olney is famous for its pancake race, where local women make pancakes on the first ring of the church bell and race on the second, dressed in aprons and headscarves. They have to toss the pancake three times.

Buckinghamshire Stokenchurch Pie is a good supper dish, made with macaroni, hardboiled eggs, and any leftover cooked meat. Mix the macaroni with the meat, place half in a pastry lined pie dish, add the eggs, and then cover with the rest of the meat and a pastry lid and bake for half an hour.

Cliveden ★★★★★ ◉◉◉

☎ 01628 668561
🅕 01628 661837
**🅔 reservations@clivedenhouse.
  co.uk**

Map ref 3 - SU98
Cliveden Estate, TAPLOW, SL6 0JF
*M4 J7, follow A4 towards Maidenhead
for 1.5m, turn onto B476 towards
Taplow, 2.5m hotel on left*
🍵 Open daily; please telephone for details of tea times and prices
🛏 39 rooms, S from £250, D from £250

A wonderful stately home in a glorious setting, where visitors are treated as house guests. From the moment you enter the quarter-mile gravel drive and pass the amazing 'Fountain of Love', you know this is going to be a very special experience. Greeted by uniformed footmen at the door, you're shown into the wonderfully atmospheric, oak-panelled Great Hall. Guests are offered a choice of rooms in which to take tea, served promptly on perfectly matching Spode china. A tempting selection of well-filled sandwiches, assorted teacakes, scones and home-made jam and pastries are available as well as a choice of tea, coffee and infusions. Guests are asked about special dietary requirements on booking.

Winner of The Tea Guild's Top Country House Hotel Award 2004.

RECOMMENDED IN THE AREA
Windsor; Henley on Thames and Regatta; Eton

Cheshire

Cheshire cheese is the oldest of our cheeses with a slightly salty tang from the soil of the Cheshire salt marshes. Cheshire makes a delicious Welsh rarebit and is also very good in potted cheese. Traditionally, the cheese is grated, mixed with butter and spice, moistened with a splash of sherry or brandy, and beaten thoroughly until smooth. The mixture is firmly pressed into small pots, sealed with melted butter and kept in the fridge. Potted cheese is delicious spread on toast for tea.

A speciality of the county town is Chester pudding – a pastry case with a frangipane-type filling and a meringue topping.

*T*he Chester Crabwall Manor Hotel ★★★★ ◉◉

With its towers and gardens, a very English place for tea

☎ 01244 851666
🖷 01244 851400
✉ crabwall@marstonhotels.com
🌐 www.marstonhotels.com

Map ref 5 - SJ46

Parkgate Road, Mollington, CHESTER, CH1 6NE
NW off A540.
☕ Open daily; Tea served 2pm-5.30pm; Closed 25-Dec; Booking possible; Set tea price(s) £12.95; Seats 20; No Smoking; No dogs; Parking 50
🛏 48 Rooms; S £151, D £181

A charming country house hotel dating from the 1660s, with a splendid castellated red brick frontage complete with towers. There has been a dwelling on the site since before Domesday, and the present hotel stands in 11 acres of beautiful mature gardens and woodland. With Chester just a short drive away, this is an ideal setting for afternoon tea in the country. Choose one of the cosy lounges, the drawing room or bar to indulge in delicate sandwiches, cakes, scones with clotted cream and jam, and a host of refreshing teas. Staff are on hand to make the experience memorable.

RECOMMENDED IN THE AREA

Chester Zoo; Chester Cathedral; Deva Roman Experience

Crewe Hall ★★★★ ◉◉

Magnificent and welcoming, the perfect place for tea

☎ / 🖷 01270 253333
📧 crewehall@marstonhotels.com
🌐 www.marstonhotels.com

Map ref 6 - SJ75

Weston Road, CREWE, CW1 6UZ
M6 junct 16, A500 to Crewe. Last exit at rdbt onto A5020. Ist exit at next rdbt to Crewe. Hotel 150yds on right..
🍵 Open daily; Tea served 2pm-5.30pm; Closed 25-Dec; Booking essential for Full Crewe Tea; Set tea price(s) £6.95, £9.95, £13.95; Seats 40; Air con; No dogs; Parking 100
🛏 65 Rooms; S £165-£397, D £195-£439

A former stately home, once the seat of the Earl of Crewe, standing in large grounds. Some breathtakingly beautiful features, including the chapel and the pantry, simply have to be seen, and there are guided historic tours for the curious. A Victorian architect extended the original Jacobean pile, and the Grade I listed building offers gracious reception rooms which were seemingly designed for afternoon tea. In the ornate Sheridan lounge you can try the light tea of sandwiches and speciality tea or coffee, the high tea - sandwiches, cakes, warm scones with clotted cream and jam, or the full Crewe tea (booking only).

RECOMMENDED IN THE AREA
Beeston Castle; Stapeley Water Gardens; Little Moreton Hall

Hanover International Hotel & Club ★★★★

A welcoming hotel with a good lounge menu

☎ 01925 730706
🖷 01925 730740
📧 reception.warrington@ hanover-international.com
🌐 www.hanover-international.com

Map ref 6 - SJ68

Stretton Road, Stretton, WARRINGTON, WA4 4NS
M56 junct 10, A49 to Warrington, at lights turn right to Appleton Thorn, hotel 200yds on right.
🍵 Open 8.30am-10.30pm; Tea served 12pm-5pm daily; Set tea price(s) £6.55; Seats 90; Air con; Parking 400
🛏 142 Rooms; S £115-£180, D £125-£180

*T*ravellers on the M56 can take heart as they approach Warrington, and allow themselves a detour for a highly profitable couple of hours. Their targeted destination is this comfortable modern hotel, where the spacious public rooms offer an ideal opportunity for refreshment. The lounge bar menu provides a tantalising choice of food throughout the day, from starters and main courses to tasty snacks and light meals. Should your visit occur in the afternoon, the tea menu will surely appeal: you can enjoy the full works, with a pot of tea or a cup of speciality coffee, or if that seems overwhelming, just a toasted teacake or crumpet instead.

RECOMMENDED IN THE AREA
Arley Hall; Tatton Park; Cheshire Oats

County Durham

Oats are a traditional staple of the north-eastern counties, from the days before wheat was much used in these parts, and oat cuisine is still reflected in the region's recipes. Durham pikelets are a kind of pancake popular for tea. They are made from a batter mixture of flour, buttermilk and bicarbonate of soda, fried and served hot with butter and jam.

Monthly farmers' markets flourish within the county at Barnard Castle, Darlington, Durham, Stanhope and Sedgefield, and are good places to check out the local specialities, including home-made cakes and bread.

*T*he Market Place Teashop

Tasty teas and lunches at reasonable prices

☎ **01833 690110**

Map ref 7 - NZ11

29 Market Place, BARNARD CASTLE, DL12 8NE

🍽 Open 10am-5.30pm Mon-Sat, 2.30-5.30pm Sun (Mar-Nov); Tea served all day; Closed 24 Dec-6 Jan; Seats 44

A charming tea shop, full of character with its 17th-century flagstones, bare stone walls and open fireplace. In previous lives it was a pub, and a gentleman's outfitters kitting out the local farm workers. Despite these rustic surroundings, tea is served in silver teapots by uniformed waitresses, and accompanied by a tempting list of goodies: meringues filled with cream and strawberries, Yorkshire curd cheesecake, fruit tarts and scones might appear on the daily-changing menu. Savoury dishes include home-made steak pie with vegetables, and prices are reasonable. The upstairs Artison shop sells chinaware, glassware, prints and original paintings.

RECOMMENDED IN THE AREA

Barnard Castle; Egglestone Abbey; Bowes Museum

41

Cornwall

Clotted cream has to be the teatime treat most closely associated with this part of the world. It has a very high fat content and is simply divine served with scones or with another local favourite, Cornish splits. These are soft buns raised with yeast, split and filled with jam and cream.

Saffron was introduced to Britain in the 14th century and soon became a popular flavouring. Crocuses were cultivated in Essex to meet the demand for saffron, which is harvested from the flower's stigma. By the early 15th century the industry in Essex was finished, but saffron continued to arrive from abroad at the Cornish ports. Thus saffron cake, bread and bun recipes remained part of the Cornish tradition, but were generally reserved for special occasions because of the extravagant nature of the critical ingredient. It takes 150,000 flowers to produce one kilogram of dried saffron!

The Cornish pasty, the tin miner's highly portable staple, is a perennial favourite, which finds continuing appeal with today's eat-on-the-move generation. The crisp ginger biscuit known as the Cornish Fairing is also still widely available, originally made to munch on fair days. Seafood is another regional speciality, and crab cakes, crab soup or a fresh crab sandwich are a delight at any time.

The Old Rectory Farm Tea Rooms

A 13th-century farmhouse just ten minutes from spectacular Cornish cliffs

☎ 01288 331251

Map ref 1 - SS21

Crosstown, Morwenstow, BUDE,
EX23 9SR

☕ Open 11am-5pm; Tea served all day daily; Closed End Sep-Etr; Booking possible; please phone to check if open outside main holiday period; Set tea price(s) please phone to check; No credit cards; Seats 30; No Smoking; No Dogs; Parking 40

*D*ating back to 1296, when it belonged to an order of monks, this working farmhouse is (not surprisingly) full of atmosphere. Heavy oak beams salvaged from wrecked ships, ancient flagstone floors worn by countless feet, and large open fireplaces with blazing logs on cold days, all help to make a visit here memorable. Speciality teas such as Gunpowder, Chai and China Oolong appear on a long list of drinks. There is a good selection of food too – everything is cooked on the premises using fresh local ingredients wherever possible. Try a Cornish cream tea with huge scones and Cornish clotted cream or a Ploughman's with a good selection of Cornish cheese, chutney and coleslaw. Also cakes, soups and pasties. Vegetarians and children catered for. Some produce and crafts on sale.

RECOMMENDED IN THE AREA
Hartland Abbey; Clovelly; Milky Way Adventure Park

Muffins

An award-winning tea shop serving varied meals and teas

☎ 01208 872278

Map ref 1 - SX16

32 Fore Street, LOSTWITHIEL,
PL22 0BN
Off A390 in main street of Lostwithiel.
☕ Open 10am-5pm; Tea served all day; Closed Sun (except in high summer, ring for dates) Jan; Booking possible; Set tea price(s) fr £3.00; Seats 24; No Smoking; Dogs in the garden only

*I*n summer a lovely walled cottage garden is just the place for afternoon tea. At other times the light and spacious tea shop with its pretty tablecloths and pine furniture is a magnet for tourists. Parts of Lostwithiel date from the late 13th century, but Muffins has moved with the times and serves a variety of tasty meals throughout the day, based where possible on fresh local produce. The Cornish Cream Teas are hard to beat, with their delicious Trewithen clotted cream and strawberry jam, or you can try the famous home-made muffins. You can buy food and gifts to take home.

The Tea Guild Award of Excellence 2004.

RECOMMENDED IN THE AREA
Eden Project; Lost Gardens of Heligan; Lanhydrock

43

WALK

The Looe River Valleys by Rail and Ramble

A short journey by rail leads to a leisurely walk along country lanes and riverside paths

This walk begins with a short, stress-free train ride from busy Looe to the serenity of Causeland Station Halt in the valley of the East Looe River. On leaving the station, turn immediately left along a quiet lane to a junction with another lane opposite Badham Farm Holiday Cottages. Brace yourself for a stiff climb for the next 0.25 miles (400m). The effort is worth it; you gain height and then the rest of the route is generally downhill all the way. In 0.75 miles (1.2km) go left over a stone stile, turn right through a gap and then head diagonally across a field towards the opposite right-hand corner and a row of houses. (If the field is under crops and no right-of-way apparent, you may have to go round the field edge). Go through a gap in the far hedge, just left of the field corner, then turn right and go through a field gate and down a lane to the main

road. Opposite is the post office and village shop. Go left along the footway to reach the welcoming Olde Plough House Inn. Continue along the main road from the pub and in about 275yds (251m) you'll reach a signpost indicating the way to the Duloe Stone Circle. This haunting Bronze Age ceremonial site is composed of eight quartzite stones, each one representing the main points of the compass. Once back on the main road, walk the few paces to Duloe's Church of St Cuby. Leave the churchyard by the top gateway into the lane alongside the village war memorial. Turn right and follow the lane, past the village green and school, for 0.75 miles (1.2km). Keep ahead past a junction on the right and descend steeply into the wooded valley of the West Looe River. Go left at a T-junction. Just before reaching the river, go left over a stile by a gate. Do not follow the track directly ahead; instead bear right at a signpost and follow a grassy path that becomes a broad track above the river. Follow the well-signposted riverside way for the next 0.75 miles (1.2km) in tandem with the chuckling river to reach a narrow lane at Sowden's Bridge. Turn right here, then cross the bridge and follow

the lane, ignoring side junctions but going left at a final three-way junction, signed 'Kilminorth and Watergate'. In 0.5 miles (800m), turn left by some pretty cottages into the nature reserve of Kilminorth Woods. These ancient oak woods were once 'coppiced', the trees being cut back to a stump and the resulting clusters of new shoots harvested for hedging and other uses. You can choose your route through the woods to Looe, either by following a lower riverside footpath, or the higher Giant's Hedge footpath that first climbs steeply uphill, then follows the line of the vegetated Giant's Hedge, probably a 6th-century boundary dyke that marked out the territory of a local chieftain. Both routes are - well-signposted and take you pleasantly back to Millpool car park.

DISTANCE: 6.5 miles (10.4km)
START/FINISH: Millpool car park, West Looe - half mile from Looe station
MAP: OS Map Explorer 107
TERRAIN : Fields, riverbank and woodland (can be muddy)
GRADIENT: Includes a stiff climb

*B*udock Vean, Hotel on the River ★★★★ ◉

Relax over tea in this exceptionally well-equipped hotel

☎ 01326 252100
🖷 01326 250892
✉ relax@budockvean.co.uk
🌐 www.budockvean.co.uk

Map ref 1 - SW63

MAWNAN SMITH, TR11 5LG
from A39 follow tourist signs to Trebah Gardens. 0.5m to hotel.
☕ Open daily; Tea served 3pm-5pm daily; Closed 2-24 Jan;
Booking possible; Set tea price(s) £4.95, £25.50 (Celebration Tea for Two); Seats 60; No Smoking areas; Parking 100
🛏 57 Rooms; S £66-£105, D £132-£210

A stunning location, an impressive range of leisure facilities, and award-winning cuisine – there are plenty of reasons to choose this riverside hotel for a visit. Set in 65 acres of well-tended gardens, it offers golf, swimming, tennis, snooker and a natural health spa, plus lovely places for walking. If all this sounds too hectic, another activity requires little more than raising the arm at intervals. Tea is a hallowed institution between 3 and 5pm, when the Budock Vean Cream Tea – think scones with clotted cream, jam and cakes, or the Celebration tea – the above with sandwiches and champagne, offer the perfect excuse for sitting down.

RECOMMENDED IN THE AREA
Trebah Gardens; Glendurgan Gardens; National Maritime Museum

---

*T*he Plantation

Victorian tea room near Polperro harbour

☎ 01503 272223
✉ plantation73@hotmail.com
🌐 www.cornwallexplore.co.uk

Map ref 1 - SX25

The Coombes, POLPERRO, PL13 2RG
☕ Open 11am-9.30pm; Tea served all day; Closed Nov-Easter; Booking possible; Set tea price(s) £3.75; Seats 50 + 70 outside

S troll down through Polperro towards the harbour, and you will be delighted to discover an award-winning tea room on the banks of the River Pol. The walls are decorated with novelty teapots, plates, jugs and biscuit barrels to emphasise its purpose, and old beams, bow windows and a real fireplace with copper canopy add to the quaint atmosphere.

The Cornish cream teas, home-made cakes and good choice of speciality teas including Green Gunpowder and Japanese Green Leaf are the perfect tonic for any afternoon.

Lunchtime specials including local fish, and Mediterranean dishes and vegetarian favourites extend the range.

RECOMMENDED IN THE AREA
Looe Monkey Sanctuary; Lanreath Farm & Folk Museum; St Catherine's Castle

*T*renance Cottage
Tea Rooms & Gardens

A highly acclaimed cottage tea room with an emphasis on quality, local, home-made fare

☎ / 🖷 01637 872034
✉ robert@trenance-cottage.co.uk
🌐 www.trenance-cottage.co.uk

Map ref 1 - SW86

Trenance Cottage, Trenance Lane,
NEWQUAY, TR7 2HX
*From town centre take Edgcombe
Ave, into Trevemper Rd. Trenance
Cottage opp boating lakes.*
🍴 Open 10-30am-5pm; Tea served
all day - but telephone to check times
in winter; Closed Nov-Mar; Booking
possible; Set tea price(s) £4.75; No
credit cards; Seats 30 + 90 outside;
No Smoking

*D*ating back some 200 years, Trenance Cottage is believed to have been one of the earliest licensed tea gardens in the area. In more recent years, proprietors Bob and Judy Poole have extensively renovated the property while focusing on the tea room tradition, with background music from the 1920s through to the 50s to strike a nostalgic note. They also offer bed and breakfast accommodation in three rooms. Trenance Cottage is a member of the Tea Council Guild of Tea Shops, and the menu lists a wide choice of teas and tisanes. Other house specialities are fresh local crab and smoked mackerel, locally grown strawberries, home-baked Cornish pasties, cream teas with local clotted cream, and locally made strawberry conserve. Light lunches, including home-made soup, ploughman's and Welsh rarebit, are served, plus a range of Cornish wines, beers and ciders during licensing hours. Some parking space is provided, and it is usually easy to park in adjacent roads. Preserves, tea and biscuits can be bought to take away. Dogs are permitted outside. Trenance Cottage has won many awards over the years including The Tea Guild's Top Tea Place 2001 and 2002, and **The Tea Guild Award of Excellence 2004.**

RECOMMENDED IN THE AREA
The Gannel River; Eden Project; Newquay Zoo

Charlotte's Tea House

Fresh home-cooked food, speciality leaf teas, and peace

☎ 01872 263706

Map ref 1 - SW65

Coinage Hall, 1 Boscawen Street,
TRURO, TR1 2QU
Town centre next to War Memorial.
☕ Open 10am-5pm; Tea served all
day; Closed Sun & BHs;
Booking possible; Set tea price(s)
£6.50; No credit cards; Seats 50;
No Smoking; No Dogs

This lovingly-restored Victorian tea house in the centre of busy Truro provides a peaceful sanctuary from the traffic noise. In these elegant surroundings, the tasteful menu offers an irresistible variety of toasted and plain sandwiches, omelettes, jacket potatoes and salads (to name just some of the choices). The good news is that the delicious set teas – cream teas with scones and high teas with sandwiches and home-made cakes – are served all day. You could choose to order China Yunnan, Jasmine or the Charlotte house blend with a toasted teacake, muffin or crumpet; coffee drinkers are rewarded with their own list of specialities. Try a champagne breakfast!

The Tea Guild Award of Excellence 2004.

RECOMMENDED IN THE AREA
Trewithen Garden; Maritime Museum, Falmouth; Trelissick Garden

---

The Nare Hotel ★★★★ ◉

Sea views and sandwiches – an afternoon idyll

☎ 01872 501111
📠 01872 501856
✉ office@narehotel.co.uk
🌐 www.narehotel.co.uk

Map ref 1 - SW85

Carne Beach, VERYAN-IN-
ROSELAND, TR2 5PF
*from Tregony follow A3078 for approx
1.5m turn left at signpost Veryan,
through village towards sea and hotel.*
☕ Open 11am onwards; Tea served
all day; Set tea price(s) £6.50;
'Quarterdeck' tea £25 for 2; Seats 70;
No smoking areas; Parking 80
🛏 38 Rooms; S £76-£145,
D £152-£290

Some settings are just made for afternoon tea, and this is surely one of them. The stunning sea views from this family-run hotel are simply breathtaking, with Gerrans Bay and Nare Head just asking to be admired. Inside the gracious, country-house style public rooms, equally marvellous flower arrangements draw the eye. For those who have walked the coastal path over National Trust land, the tea menu is a treat indeed. Go for the classic Cornish Cream Tea of scones, clotted cream and jam, or the more extensive Quarterdeck choice, both washed down with a decent choice of tea. For slighter appetites, a home-made biscuit and cuppa are also served.

RECOMMENDED IN THE AREA
The Eden Project; National Maritime Museum; Lost Gardens of Heligan

*T*he Tea Shop

Charming tea rooms serving only home-made food

☎ 01208 813331

Map ref 1 - SW07

6 Polmorla Road, WADEBRIDGE, PL27 7ND

🍵 Open 10am-4.30pm; Tea served all day; Closed Sun & BHs, 25, 26 Dec, 1 Jan; Booking possible; Cream tea price(s) £3.20; No credit cards; Seats 22; No Smoking

*F*resh local produce takes pride of place on the menu at this bright and cosy tea shop, and everything served here is home-made. This proud boast comes from owner Nicky Ryland, whose support of the town is amply repaid by the regular customers attracted by her delicious food. A selection of 40 teas makes her a winner with visitors to the area too, with around 30 cakes including boiled fruit cake, strawberry pavlova, and apple and almond cake always available. Ice creams are another favourite, and there are light lunches such as jacket potatoes and salads for those whose intentions are less frivolous. A highchair is available, and there is wheelchair access.

The Tea Guild Award of Excellence 2004.

RECOMMENDED IN THE AREA
Coastal walks; Camel Trail; Pencarrow House

Cumbria

Cumbria is a county rich in traditional recipes. Well-known foods include Cumberland sausage, a long, thin sausage usually presented coiled on the plate, and Cumberland sauce, made with thickened redcurrant jelly, port and citrus fruit, and served with ham, venison and lamb.

Cumberland rum butter, a hard sauce of butter, brown sugar and rum, is at the heart of a charming old custom. Visitors to see a newborn baby were given rum butter and oatcakes to eat and in turn would leave a silver coin. On the day of the christening, when the butter bowl had been emptied, it would be used to hold the coins. A bowl with plenty of buttery coins sticking to it would augur well for the baby's future prosperity.

Kendal mint cake (much more of a sweet than a cake) has been made in the town since 1869, and famously sustained Sir Edmund Hillary and Tensing Norgay during their successful assault on Mount Everest in 1953. Legend has it that they stopped for a nibble at the summit. Mint cake remains an indispensable addition to the fell walker's rations – light to carry and packed with energy. Grasmere gingerbread is another old favourite, much more like shortbread to eat than any other kind of ginger cake (or bread). Like Kendal mint cake, it is still made and sold locally.

Armathwaite Hall ★★★★ ◉

A stately home set in 400 acres with exceptional views of Bassenthwaite Lake and Skiddaw Mountain

☎ 017687 76551
📠 017687 76220
✉ reservations@
armathwaite-hall.com
🌐 www.armathwaite-hall.com

Map ref 5 - NY23
BASSENTHWAITE, CA12 4RE
M6 junct 40/A66 to Keswick rdbt then A591 signed Carlisle. 8m to Castle Inn junct, turn left. Hotel 300yds.
🍽 Open daily; Tea served 2pm-5pm daily; Closed 25 Dec & 1 Jan; Booking advisable on BH weekends; Set tea price(s) £9.95; Seats 70; Smoking in Hall Lounge only; Parking 100
🛏 43 Rooms; S £70-£150, D £140-£280

*I*nviting public rooms with roaring log fires, fine art and antique pieces are just part of the appeal of this impressive stone-built, 17th-century mansion. The hotel enjoys a stunning location on Bassenthwaite Lake, surrounded by its own extensive deer park and woodland, amid Lakeland fells in an area beloved of William Wordsworth. Country house traditions are proudly upheld at Armathwaite Hall, and not least among them is the splendid afternoon tea served in the Lake Room or Hall Lounge. The full meal comprises a selection of sandwiches, scones, jam and cream, cakes and biscuits – all home-made. There is a good choice of sandwiches, toasties or pannini rolls, though guests can simply opt for strawberries and cream, or a fres cream meringue or éclair. This is a popular treat s booking is advisable on bank holiday weekends The Hall offers full hotel facilities, including the Sp Leisure Club and outdoor pursuits. No dogs.

RECOMMENDED IN THE AREA
Bowness-on-Windermere; Trotters World of Animals; Keswick Launch on Derwent Water

Hazelmere Café and Bakery

A tea-lover's heaven, with delicious food to match

☎ 01539 532972
✉ hazelmeregrange@yahoo.co.uk

Map ref 5 - SD97

1 Yewbarrow Terrace,
GRANGE OVER SANDS, LA11 6ED
From A590 take B5277 into Grange-over-Sands. Pass the station, then 1st left at mini rdbt. Hazelmere is 1st two properties on right.
☕ Open 10am-4.30pm (winter) 10am-5pm (summer); Tea served all day; Closed 25 & 26 Dec & 1 Jan; Booking possible; Seats 50 + 30 upstairs; No Smoking

*E*xpect at least 28 different types of tea from all around the world at this award-winning tea shop. Praise has been heaped on it for the variety and quality of its 'cuppas', as well as the range of freshly-made and locally-sourced meals and snacks that are served here. Bread, cakes, chutneys, pâtés and preserves are all baked on the premises, and offered alongside local pheasant burger, Cumbria lamb tattie pot, and Murghal chicken. Teatime specialities include Cumberland Rum Nicky, vanilla slices, and scones made with apricot and yoghurt, and the large gracious tea room with its open fire or summer verandah can be found in a handsome Victorian arcade.

The Tea Guild Award of Excellence 2004.

RECOMMENDED IN THE AREA
Holker Hall & Gardens; Levens Hall; Aquarium of the Lakes

Wordsworth Hotel ★★★★ ◎◎

A stone-built Victorian property in a lovely Lake District village

☎ 015394 35592
📠 015394 35765
✉ enquiry@ wordsworth-grasmere.co.uk
🌐 www.grasmere-hotels.co.uk

Map ref 5 - NY30

GRASMERE, LA22 9SW
centre of village adjacent to St Oswald's Church.
☕ Open daily; Tea served 3.30pm-5.15pm daily; Booking possible; Seats 25-30; No smoking areas; Air con; Parking 60
🛏 37 Rooms; S £120-£200, D £190-£300

*T*he Wordsworth is a privately owned, traditional hotel set in two acres of award-winning gardens. Public rooms are furnished with antiques and afford splendid views of the surrounding landscape that once inspired the Lakeland poet. Tea can be served in the conservatory, small lounge, or out in the garden. A set cream tea is available or an afternoon tea of cucumber and egg mayonnaise sandwiches, home-made scones with jam and whipped cream, and a selection of the hotel's own cakes. The hotel has its own pub next door, The Dove & Olive Branch, where snacks and light meals are served. Dogs are permitted in the garden, and parking is provided.

RECOMMENDED IN THE AREA
Dove Cottage & Museum (Wordsworth's Home); Grasmere Lake; Heaton Coopers Art Gallery

51

WALK

A Round of Rydal Water

A circuit of Rydal Water via Loughrigg Terrace and the Coffin Route

From the higher car park, walk above the road, cross the road and descend the steps which lead across the common to gain the track by the river. If you start in the car park below the road, beyond the low barrier, take the track into the wood. Cross a footbridge and continue until the track nears the river. The two paths from both car parks lead to this point. Pass the bend in the river and continue along the track to bear left. Cross the footbridge over the river. Take the path straight on, through the woods away from the river. Ascend to a kissing gate leading to a stony track. At this point an alternative route bears left by the shoreline of Rydal Water. Take the path above, which bears left to ascend through the bracken to a level path known as Loughrigg Terrace. Traverse left along the path to a fine viewpoint, overlooking the lake, and on to Nab Cottage

and Nab Scar. Continue along the path to round the next shoulder and cross a level area of slate waste. Beyond this, find the entrance to Rydal Cave, an old slate quarry. Descend the track directly below this and pass through a larch wood before the track bears right to pass a further quarry hole and caves. Keep along the track, which rounds a little bend before becoming a walled lane that descends between Jobson Close, below, and the woods of Rough Intake, above. Intercept a track and cross it, bearing left slightly, to find a path down to Rydal Water. Bear right to enter woods by a gate. The path leads through the wood and then, with the lake just over to the left, walk through the field to intercept the River Rothay. Cross by the bridge on to the A591. The Badger Bar stands opposite. Bear right along the road until a lane leads uphill to the left. Cross the road and follow the lane up to Rydal church and Dora's Field, then steeper still to pass by Rydal Mount, the home of William Wordsworth. Immediately above Rydal Mount a track bears left. Pass through a gate and follow this track, the old Coffin Route which runs between Ambleside and Grasmere. Stony in places,

the track is well defined, traversing through clumps of oaks with a view south over Rydal Water. As the track rounds a bend and intercepts a wall there is a square stone on the right. This is the coffin rest stone, where the bearers once placed their burden for a breather. There is a seat beyond this and then a gate leads through a wall and the track enters the woods above Nab Cottage. Keep along the track and pass through a gate, to dip slightly, before making a short steep ascent. The wall above on the right at this point is an exposed part of the Thirlmere Aqueduct, which runs all the way to Manchester. Round the shoulder and make a rocky descent to cross a stream. Keep on to a gate below a house above the track to the right. Through this gate a lane falls steeply down the hillside to the left. Take this lane through the wood to intercept the A591 just above the lower car park at White Moss Common.

DISTANCE: 3 miles (4.8km) 1hr 30min
START/FINISH: Grid Reference SD 348066 Car Park, White Moss Common
MAP: OS Explorer OL 7
TERRAIN : Woodland vale beneath high fells - stony paths and tracks
GRADIENT: Some steep sections

*L*akeside Hotel ★★★★ ◎◎

A relaxing lakeside conservatory serving an interesting range of hot and cold snacks and a choice of afternoon teas

☎ 015395 30001
✆ 015395 31699
✉ sales@lakesidehotel.co.uk
🌐 www.lakesidehotel.co.uk

Map ref 5 - SD38

Lakeside, NEWBY BRIDGE, LA12 8AT
M6 junct 36 join A590 to Barrow, take signs to Newby Bridge. Right over bridge, hotel 1m on right or follow Lakeside Steamers signs from junct 36.

☕ Tea served 3pm-5pm daily; Closed 23 Dec-2 Jan; Set tea price(s) £23.00 (two people); Seats 30; Parking 200
🛏 80 Rooms; S £110-£275, D £140-£280

A conservatory looking out across landscaped gardens to Lake Windermere beyond makes a charming setting for afternoon tea. This impressive hotel, richly decorated and sumptuously furnished, has moved a long way from its origins as a 17th-century coaching inn offering hospitality to passing traffic. Nowadays a menu of open sandwiches (Coronation chicken, grilled vegetables and mozzarella), hot dishes like pan-fried salmon, and three cheese tortellini, plus such desserts as Eton mess and sticky toffee pudding, greet visitors looking for a light repast for lunch and throughout the afternoon. A full afternoon tea – expect a feast of sandwiches, cakes, toasted fruit bread, strawberries, scones and fresh cream – will satisfy hearty appetites, while a more modest choice of scones, crumpets or cakes with tea is also appealing. Speciality teas join a popular selection of coffees, hot chocolate and fresh orange juice, and there is also a short wine list. A luxury spa will help to work off the calories afterwards!

RECOMMENDED IN THE AREA

Windermere Lake Cruisers; Lakeside & Haverthwaite Steam Railway; Aquarium of the Lakes

New Village Tea Rooms

Converted cottage with coal fire and summer umbrellas

☎ / ℱ 01539 624886

Map ref 6 - NY52

Orton, PENRITH, CA10 3RH
☕ Open daily; Tea served 10am-5pm
Apr-Oct, 10.30am-4.30pm Nov-Mar;
Closed 25, 26 Dec, 1 Jan; Booking
possible; Set tea prices(s) £6.50; No
credit cards; Seats 22 + extra outside
in summer; No Smoking; Dogs
allowed in garden only; Parking 5

An 18th-century building with a varied history that has most recently been used as a cottage. The open-plan arrangement downstairs means that visitors enjoying a meal can chat to the kitchen staff, and feel really at home. In winter an open coal fire keeps the place cosy, and creates a welcome refuge for walkers; in summer the tea rooms remain cool on hot days, while sun lovers can take themselves into the pretty garden to bask. Locally-produced quality ingredients go into the home-cooked menu, with its irresistible cakes, desserts, sandwiches and hot lunches, plus a choice of interesting teas.

The Tea Guild Award of Excellence 2004

RECOMMENDED IN THE AREA
Wetheriggs Country Pottery; Dalemain; Brougham Castle

Derbyshire

Derbyshire's best-known speciality is probably the Bakewell tart, known and appreciated across the world, though locals would remind you of its original and proper title, the Bakewell pudding. The first Bakewell pudding, dating from about 1860, was actually a culinary accident. A visiting nobleman to one of the town's coaching inns (now the Rutland Arms) ordered a strawberry tart. The inn's hapless cook accidentally poured the egg mixture over the jam, but the result was so pleasing that she was urged to keep producing the puddings in this way. The Bakewell pudding is just as popular in Bakewell today, but the original recipe is still a closely guarded secret.

Derbyshire is also a successful cheese-making county. The Derby cheese always rather suffered from its similarity to the more popular Cheddar, but during the 17th century the addition of chopped sage leaves to the curd (for its perceived health-giving properties) created the distinctive sage Derby. The cheese has subsequently been presented in various ways, with a 'sandwich filling' of sage running through the middle, or with an attractive green marbled effect, more popular these days, created by the addition of spinach juice to the sage leaves. A fine Stilton cheese is also made in Derbyshire, in the village of Hartington.

Ashbourne in Derbyshire is believed to be the birthplace of the gingerbread man, first created by a French prisoner who made his home in the town after the Napoleonic wars. His recipe has been handed down through the generations, and the gingerbread men are still proudly made today.

*N*orthern Tea Merchants

Excellent teas to sample with the traditional afternoon accompaniments, or to buy from a wide specialist range

☎ 01246 233243
✉ enquiries@northern-tea.com
🖥 www.northern-tea.com

Map ref 8 - SK37

Crown House, 193 Chatsworth Road,
CHESTERFIELD, S40 2BA
One mile from centre of Chesterfield on A619 (road to Chatsworth House).

☕ Open Mon-Fri 9am-5pm, Sat 9am-4.30pm; Tea served all day; Closed Sun & BHs; Booking possible; Set tea price(s) £5.50; Seats 20; No Smoking; Guide dogs only; Parking 16

*T*his tea and coffee tasting bar is owned and run by a company of tea merchants – it doesn't get much more specialist than this! A family firm of tea blenders and tea bag manufacturers, which supplies stately homes and restaurants with their favourite brew, offers casual visitors the chance to sample the same high quality. From Formosa Oolong and Ceylon Orange Pekoe to Russian Caravan and a range of flavoured teas, each one is clearly described, and served on its own or with a traditional afternoon accompaniment like cucumber sandwiches, home-made cake, or scone with jam and cream. The less exotic teas and a choice of five house blends are also listed, along with a mouthwatering array of pure Arabica coffee beans. Light meals and snacks, such as filled jacket potatoes, ploughman's lunch, salads and sandwiches are served throughout the day. Tours of the premises and tea tastings can be arranged, and there's a shop selling tea caddies, teapots and of course tea!

The Tea Guild Award of Excellence 2004.

RECOMMENDED IN THE AREA

Chatsworth House; Hardwick House; Crooked Spire of St Mary and All Saints Church

Devon

Devon is renowned for the quality and abundance of its locally produced food: fresh fish and seafood from its coastal waters and a wide range of produce from its lush farmlands, including some notable organic suppliers. Devon's dairy produce is legendary: rich, creamy milk crafted into fine farmhouse cheeses, butter, ice creams, yoghurts and thick, golden clotted cream.

The Devon cream tea is a grand tradition, widely enjoyed in tea rooms across the county, featuring scones, butter, jam and clotted cream. Cream also makes its appearance in the Devon split, a yeasted bun, split and filled with jam and cream. Clotted cream is also the magic ingredient in Devon flats, a mixture of flour, sugar and clotted cream creating something between a scone and a biscuit. Another local speciality is Devon apple cake, a fruity, spicy, buttery mixture with a lovely crumble topping. Farmers' markets are flourishing and are a regular feature of the county's towns, large or small. They are a great place to get a taste of locally produced and hand made foods, including cakes, breads, preserves and pickles. Local cheeses to look out for are Beenleigh Blue, Devon Garland (garlanded with oregano and spring onion), and the Sharpham range. Devon is also an excellent honey-producing area, so don't miss out on the sticky stuff.

Cosy Tea Pot
A small teashop with a huge reputation

☎ / 🖷 01395 444016

Map ref 2 - SY18

13 Fore Street, BUDLEIGH SALTERTON,
EX9 6NH
*From High Street towards seafront, tea shop
opposite The Creamery.*
☕ Open Tue-Sun; Tea served Winter Tue-Sat
10.30am-4.30pm, Sun 11am-4.30pm;
summer Tue-Sat 10am-5pm, Sun 11am-5pm;
Closed Mondays; Booking possible;
Set cream tea price(s) £2.75, £3.50; No credit
cards; Seats 36; No Smoking; Air conditioned
in summer; Guide dogs only

Cross a small bridge over the babbling Budleigh
Brook to reach this charming Victorian-style tea
rooms. If you arrive at lunchtime you can expect
various light lunches including daily specials. In
winter months there are special Thursday set
lunches, and Sunday roasts by prior booking.
Afternoon tea is the strongest lure, however, and it is
easy to see why. Wonderful home-made cakes,
scones and biscuits are always on show, along with
the Devonshire Cream Tea, and the Teacake special.
Your choice of speciality tea is served from fine
Royal Albert china next to vases of fresh flowers on
lacy white tablecloths, by smart and friendly staff.

Open fires add to the period atmosphere and
comfortable surroundings.

RECOMMENDED IN THE AREA
*Powderham Castle; Killerton House & Garden;
Fairlynch Museum, Budleigh Salterton*

Northcote Manor ★★★ ◎◎
18th-century manor house in a lovely North Devon location

☎ 01769 560501
🖷 01769 560770
✉ rest@northcotemanor.co.uk
🌐 www.northcote-manor.com

Map ref 2 - SS61

BURRINGTON, EX37 9LZ
*off A377 opp Portsmouth Arms, into
hotel drive. Do not enter Burrington
village.*
☕ Open daily; Tea served 2.30pm-
6pm; Closed when guests reserve
'exclusive use';
Booking advisable at weekends; Set
tea price(s) £5.75, £10.50;
No Smoking; Parking 30
🛏 11 Rooms; S £99-£165,
D £140-£235

Set at the end of a winding, wooded driveway is this
stone-built country house, dating from 1716. It is
surrounded by 20 acres of mature gardens, lawns and
woodlands and affords wonderful views over the Taw Valley.
You can take your tea by an open log fire in the hotel lounge
or Oak Room, or sit outside in fine weather. The menu offers
light meals, salads and sandwiches, a Devon cream tea with
lashings of clotted cream, and a full afternoon tea with a
round of sandwiches, scones with jam and cream, fruit
teacake, shortbread and ginger biscuits.
Booking is advisable at weekends. Dogs
permitted.

RECOMMENDED IN THE AREA
*RHS Rosemoor Gardens; Arlington Court
(National Trust); Dartington Crystal*

WALK

From Sidford on the A3052 follow signs for Sidmouth and Fortescue. After a few minutes park safely on the broad road near the phone box on the left. A footpath sign ahead directs you right, down a path to a kissing gate into the grassy meadows by the Sid. Cross the river via a wooden footbridge, then turn left. The path veers away from the river, passes through a kissing gate, and along the field edge to a crossroads of footpaths. Go left to pass a beautiful wildflower meadow on the left. This is Gilchrist Field Nature Reserve, owned and managed by the Sid Vale Association, who aim 'to protect the natural history and wildlife of the area'. Follow the path on to rejoin the river by a small weir. Just past some pretty cottages (right) cross the wooden footbridge over the river and turn right to enter The Byes, parkland with splendid mature trees. Keep straight on, passing two footbridges.

Just after the next weir leave The Byes through a white metal gate to meet the road by The Byes Toll House, built in early 19th-century Greek revival style. Cross over and down Millford Road, over the river via a wooden footbridge at a ford, and down Mill Street. Turn first left (Riverside Road); when that turns sharp right keep straight on past the children's playground to the seafront. Turn right to walk along Sidmouth's seafront past delightful Regency –terraces, bedecked with hanging baskets in summer. The long banks of 'boulders' rising from the sea here are part of Sidmouth's sea defences, constructed in the early 1990s to prevent further storm erosion. Pass the Bedford Hotel, on the right, and carry on to the end of the promenade. Follow signs for Connaught Gardens along the narrow Clifton Walkway at the back of the beach. Note: Don't walk here in heavy sea

conditions; leave the seafront and continue left uphill away from the town to reach Connaught Gardens (left). The walkway leads under the edge of the marl cliff to overlook the beach at Jacob's Ladder, with lovely views to Peak Hill. Turn round and almost immediately climb the metal-railed and very steep steps left up the cliff. Turn left up more steps into Connaught Gardens under an arch. Walk through the gardens away from the sea to the road, turning right downhill to rejoin the promenade. Wander back along the seafront, left up the river, over the footbridge at the ford, and back into The Byes. For a change of scene cross the first footbridge and walk up the left bank of the Sid. Go straight past the bridge on which you originally crossed the river and retrace your steps to your car.

DISTANCE: 3.75 miles (6km)
1hr 30min
START/FINISH: Grid Reference SY 137891 Phone box on A3052 alongside the Sid
TOTAL ASCENT: Negligible
MAP: OS Explore 115
TERRAIN : Meadows, town park and seafront
GRADIENT: Level

*T*illy's Tea Room

A charming tea room just three minutes from the seafront

RECOMMENDED IN THE AREA
Powderham Castle; Bradley Manor; Canonteign Falls

☎ **01626 889999**

Map ref 2 - SX98

2 Piermont Place, DAWLISH, EX7 9PQ
On main Exeter road, opposite Tourist Information Centre.

☕ Open 10am-5pm; Tea served all day; Closed Sun & Mon, various weeks in winter, please telephone for details; Booking possible; Set tea price(s) £3.75; No credit cards; Seats 28; No Smoking

*T*he wonderful aroma of fresh tea and coffee and home-made cakes is a temptation which few passers-by on their way to Dawlish's seafront can resist. This attractive Victorian property has been restored and redecorated in period style by its enthusiastic owners, and now features pretty table settings with fresh flowers, and fine bone china tea sets. Surrounded by a nostalgic collection of old photographs, farm tools and advertising signs, visitors can tuck into light lunches like Welsh rarebit, and gorgeous cream teas, with a range of drinks including green tea, redbush, camomile, Earl Grey and Assam providing instant refreshment.

---

*S*ir George Newnes Tearooms

Traditional cream teas and friendly service

☎ **01598 753478**

Map ref 2 - SS74

14 Lee Road, LYNTON, EX35 6HW
A39 to Lynton. Tearoom opposite Town Hall in Lee Road (main street).
☕ Open 10am-5pm (Summer), 9.30am-4pm (Winter); Tea served all day; Closed Mon (Summer), Mon & Tues (Winter), 1st week Jan; Booking possible; Set cream tea price(s) from £3.45; Seats 34; No Smoking; Guide dogs only

*L*ynton is set in beautiful countryside in the Exmoor National Park, in an area known as 'Little Switzerland'. The Sir George Newnes Tea Rooms, named after a Victorian journalist and philanthropist who left money to the Lynton cliff railway, can be found opposite the unusual Town Hall building. Delicious cakes and light lunches can be enjoyed in this charming establishment, which is adorned with hanging baskets during the summer. The Ginger Cream tea, served with honey and clotted cream, is the speciality here, and a wide choice of tea is available to accompany it, including Assam, Kenya, Earl Grey, Darjeeling, Lapsang Soochong, and Ceylon, as well as herbal teas. The Pixie tea (one scone with jam or honey and clotted cream) is for those with smaller appetites.

RECOMMENDED IN THE AREA
Valley of Rocks; Cliff Railway, Lynmouth

*T*he Clock Tower Tearooms

A remarkable cliff-top building overlooking the sea

☎ 01395 512477
✉ frasersds.150.fsnet.co.uk

Map ref 2 - SY18

Connaught Gardens, Peak Hill Road,
SIDMOUTH, EX10 8RZ
☕ Open 10am-5pm; Tea served all
day; Set tea price(s) £3.80;
Visa/Switch only; Seats 52;
No Smoking

*T*here are fabulous sea views from this extraordinary establishment on the cliffs at Sidmouth, which has been carved out of what was once part of a lime kiln. Attractive gardens and a conservatory providing additional seating are all part of the attraction. The regular menu of freshly cut sandwiches, toasties, jacket potatoes and ploughmans is supplemented by a daily blackboard menu of hot and cold dishes, such as home-made lasagne or cottage pie. House specialities are the home-made cakes, scones and gateaux, and the ultimate hot chocolate, plus a set cream tea.

Children and dogs are welcome, and books and postcards are offered for sale.

RECOMMENDED IN THE AREA
South West Coast Path, Otterton Mill Centre, The Donkey Sanctuary

*H*otel Riviera ★★★★ ◉

A hospitable seaside hotel where tea is taken very seriously

☎ 01395 515201
📠 01395 577775
✉ enquiries@hotelriviera.co.uk
⊕ www.hotelriviera.co.uk

Map ref 2 - SY18

The Esplanade, SIDMOUTH,
EX10 8AY
M5 junct 30 & follow A3052.

☕ Tea served 3pm-5.30pm daily;
No Dogs; Parking 26
🛏 27 Rooms; S £100-£132,
D £180-£244 (room rates include full
breakfast, 7-course dinner & VAT)

*T*his delightful Regency hotel overlooks the sea; old-fashioned service and modern comforts share a prominent place on the agenda. In a town once patronised by royalty, it comes as no surprise to find that taking afternoon tea in sumptuous surroundings remains a revered and celebrated practice. Between the hours of 3 and 5.30, the delicate tinkling of silver on bone china can be heard in the lounge and foyer, and on the patio in fine weather. The choice is between the Devon Cream Tea, the Strawberry Cream Tea, and the Traditional Afternoon selection, with one of six speciality teas prepared expertly to suit your mood.

RECOMMENDED IN THE AREA
Exeter Cathedral; Killerton House & Gardens; Beer Quarry Caves

*T*he Corn Dolly

A wide choice of sweet and savoury teas, with old favourites for children

☎ 01769 574249
✆ 01398 341695

Map ref 2 - SS72

115a East Street, SOUTH MOLTON,
EX36 3DB

🍴 Open 9.30am-5pm Mon-Sat, 11am-5pm
Sun; Tea served all day; Closed Sat,
25 Dec-2 Jan; Booking possible; Set tea
price(s) £3.95-£6.25; Seats 33; No smoking

RECOMMENDED IN THE AREA
RHS Rosemoor; Exmoor National Park; Minehead

*T*he Corn Dolly calls itself a Real Tea Shop, and there is no doubting the serious approach to the national drink, and the quality of the product served here. This relaxed and friendly tea shop, a popular meeting place for locals and a magnet for Devon's summer visitors, provides a delicious range of meals and snacks throughout the day. For lunch there are salads, filled jacket potatoes, sandwiches and tasty things on toast. Children will enjoy the Humpty Dumpty Tea of boiled egg and soldiers plus drink, or Tigger Tea of beans on toast. For adults there's a range of tea choices, like Gamekeeper's Tea – venison, duck and pheasant pâté with toast, or perhaps the Queen's Ransom of toasted crumpets with Stilton. The Corn Dolly Tea of scones, clotted cream and jam, and the Apple Pie Tea, a hearty slice with clotted cream, are sweeter versions, but all are served with a refreshing pot of loose leaf tea from an impressive choice.

The Tea Guild Award of Excellence 2004.

Some of the World's Best Teas

Speciality Teas:
• take their name from the plantation on which they are grown (usually referred to as single estate or single source teas)
• come from a particular area or country
• are blended for a particular time of day or occasion
• are blends to which flower, fruit, herb or spice flavourings have been added.

Some Teas from China

Gunpowder

A green tea which is steamed and rolled into small pellets without breaking the veins or leaf surface, and then dried. When the pellets are brewed in hot water they produce a very light, refreshing, pale-coloured tea that has a slightly grassy taste. This tea should be drunk without milk.

Chun Mee

This green tea is made from delicately curved leaves which resemble Chun Mee, or 'Precious Eyebrows'. The tea takes skill and patience to process and the long, twisty pieces of leaf give a pale yellow infusion that should have a smooth, slighty plummy taste. Like most Chinese teas, this should be taken without milk.

Jasmine

Green tea mixed with jasmine flowers. The blooms are picked during the day, but stored in a cool place until they open to release their powerful fragrance at night. Sometimes the piles of flowers and tea leaves are placed next to each other so that the tea is scented by the jasmine. Ordinary grades are scented two or three times, but the very best is perfumed seven times. Sometimes the tea and flowers are layered together in tea chests. The flowers you will find in packets of jasmine tea are not the flowers used for scenting but a decorative touch.

Keemun

Anhui Province is in the northwest of East China across the basins of the Yangtze River and the Huaihe River, and from this iron and coal producing region comes this black tea, which is confusingly referred to by the Chinese as the 'King of Red Teas'. The processing is skilled, as each tight black strip is made from one entire leaf. The infusion is a clear, rich, amber colour, and the aroma and taste are sometimes delicately scented with a hint of rose or orchid. Drink without milk.

Lapsang Souchong

A large leaf black tea distinguished by its smoky aroma and flavour. The tea is withered over pine fires, then stuffed into wooden barrels, covered with a cloth and left to oxidise. Then it is rolled, pan-fried and finally spread out into bamboo baskets and left to dry over smoking pine fires. The infusion is a rich red colour and is better drunk without milk.

Yunnan

A black tea from Yunnan Province in the south west of China, where tea is thought to have originated. The tea plants that grow in this area produce fat sturdy buds and shoots, and the leaves are thick and fleshy. Yunnan teas are very similar in appearance to Assam teas, having plenty of little golden flecks amongst the black pieces of leaf. The fairly strong, slightly peppery flavour is also similar, and this is the only Chinese tea that drinks well with a little milk.

Oolong

Chinese oolongs are mostly made in Fujian Province although some other districts now also produce them. The leaves are often quite twisted and crinkly in appearance and are usually much lighter brown than Chinese black teas. When brewed in boiling water, the leaves gradually unfurl and reveal pink-red markings mixed with the greens and browns of the semi-oxidised tea. The oolongs have wonderful names such as Ti Kwan Yin (Tea of the Iron Goddess of Mercy), Wu Yi Shui Hsien (Water Sprite), Dahongpao (Scarlet Robe), and Fonghwang Tan-Chung. These different brands are not often found in Britain, and most blends are marketed simply as 'China Oolong'. Drink without milk.

Essex

The 14th century brought a craze to Britain for the newly imported and very expensive saffron, harvested from the stigma of the crocus flower and used to flavour both sweet and savoury dishes. Growing demand inspired a whole new style of farming in Essex, where fields of crocus flowers were grown and harvested until the early 15th century, when the industry died out. The saffron era has, however, left a legacy of local recipes for saffron breads and cakes, and is still recalled in the name of the town Saffron Waldon. Essex traditionally had a variety of local breads, including Essex huffers that are still available today. These are large triangular baps made by cutting a round of dough into equal sections. Colchester is associated with both gooseberries and oysters, while Southend lays claim to cockle cakes, delicately flavoured sweet pastries cooked in a scallop shell.

*T*ea on the Green

Village green teashop with superb cakes and savouries

☎ 01245 226616
✉ mick@
    teaonthegreen.fsnet.co.uk

Map ref 4 - TL71

3 Eves Corner, DANBURY, CM3 4QF
M25 then A12 to Colchester, A414 to Maldon & Danbury.
☕ Open daily; Afternoon tea served 8.30am-4pm Mon-Fri, 10am-4pm Sat, 11am-4pm Sun; Closed at Xmas; Booking possible; Set tea price(s) £8.25; No credit cards; Seats 30; No Smoking; Guide dogs only; Parking 14

*T*eapots of all shapes and sizes on display and a collection of books on tea and coffee to peruse leave customers in no doubt about the function of this large pink building. Overlooking the village green on National Trust land, it has tables outside for summer weather, and a bright and spacious interior where fine white bone china sits on floral tablecloths. There is plenty to eat, from breakfast and light lunch choices such as filled pitta bread to a broad range of tea items: hot-buttered crumpets, muffins and cinnamon toast, finger sandwiches, scones and cakes and a choice of speciality teas.

The Tea Guild Award of Excellence 2004.

RECOMMENDED IN THE AREA
RHS Garden Hyde Hall; Mole Hall Wildlife Park; Saffron Walden Museum

*S*quires

A cosy tea and coffee shop serving delicious fresh meals

☎ 01268 741791

Map ref 4 - TQ79

11 High Street, RAYLEIGH, SS6 7EW
*From A127 take A129 into Rayleigh
High Street. Squires at very top of
High Street on right.*

☕ Open 9am-5pm; Tea served from
2pm; Closed Sun & BHs; Set tea
price(s) £6.95; No credit cards; Seats
32; No Smoking; No Dogs

*P*retty as a picture from the outside, with its twin bay windows and hanging baskets, Squires is cosy and inviting inside. Snuggling comfortably between a neighbouring period property and a more modern office building at the top of the High Street, it offers a varied all-day coffee shop menu that specialises in soups, quiches and cakes among several other dishes. To a background of mainly jazz, the set afternoon tea is served from a choice of 20 different loose leaf teas and a similar number of pure Arabica coffees, along with a variety of sandwiches, scones with cream and jam, and fresh cakes.

The Tea Guild Award of Excellence 2004.

RECOMMENDED IN THE AREA

*Hadleigh Castle; Southend Museum,
Planetarium & Discovery Centre;
Tilbury Fort*

Gloucestershire

cheese, mustard and ale is softened together in the oven (in an oven-proof dish topped with foil), and served on toasted bread.

The county also has its own take on the pre-Lenten pancake feast – Gloucestershire pancakes are made with suet and are more like fritters to eat. Lardy cake, also big in Wiltshire, is another regional favourite, a yeasted dough packed with sugar, fruit and lard – great for comfort eating.

Locally grown apples, cooked with brown sugar, are sandwiched between shortbread rounds to make another speciality – Gloucester shortcake.

A popular savoury dish is Gloucester cheese and ale, a local version of Welsh rarebit, where a mixture of double Gloucester

*T*he Queen's ★★★★

Tea remains an institution at this famous Cheltenham building

- ☎ 0870 400 8107
- 🅕 01242 224145
- 🅔 gm.queens@macdonald-hotels.co.uk
- 🅦 www.macdonaldhotels.co.uk

Map ref 2 - SO82

The Promenade, CHELTENHAM, GL50 1NN
Follow town centre signs. Left at Montpellier Walk rdbt. Entrance 500mtrs right.
☕ Tea served 10am-6pm daily; Closed 24-25 Dec; Set tea price(s) £6.95, £9.95; Seats 40 + 32 in garden; Guide dogs only; Parking 80
🛏 79 Rooms; S £145, D £149

A landmark hotel spectacularly located at the top of Cheltenham's main promenade. Afternoon tea taken here is one of the highlights of a visit to the Regency Spa town, or the surrounding Cotswold countryside. While 19th-century ladies might have taken tea in their boudoirs, the comfortable hotel lounge (and garden in summer) is deemed more suitable here.

Several classic teas are offered to accompany the Cotswold Cream Tea – scones with clotted cream and jam, and fruit or Madeira cake – or the Queen's Full Afternoon selection: various finger sandwiches, scones and cream, and cream cakes and pastries. Other full and light meals and sandwiches are served, accompanied by a short wine list.

RECOMMENDED IN THE AREA
Sudeley Castle & Gardens; Crickley Hill Country Park; Birdland Park & Gardens

The Black Cat

A combined shop and tea rooms on Lechlade's High Street

☎ 01367 252273
Ⓦ www.crown-lechlade.co.uk/blackcat

Map ref 3 - SU20

High Street, LECHLADE, GL7 3AD

☕ Open daily; Tea served 9.30am-5.30pm; Closed 25 Dec, 31 Dec, 1 Jan; Set tea price(s) £3.45; Seats 40; No smoking areas; Air con

*T*he Black Cat is a family-run business established in 18th-century stone-built premises, with a pretty patio for summer use. The business is owned by Alan and Valerie Watkins, who also run the town's Crown Inn. All the food is home-made, including all-day breakfast, daily hot dishes, snacks, sandwiches, children's meals and a popular Sunday roast. Home-made cakes are a speciality, and there is a set cream tea. The shop specialises in tea and coffee, and now also has a delicatessen counter. Merchandise extends to grinders, cafetières, teapots, mugs and other tea and coffee-related equipment, plus gifts, souvenirs and recipe books. Guide dogs only.

The Tea Guild Award of Excellence 2004.

RECOMMENDED IN THE AREA
Christmas Shop; St Lawrence Church with Shelley's Walk; River Thames and lock

The Marshmallow

Refreshment for energetic antique-shop browsers

☎ 01608 651536

Map ref 3 - SP23

High Street, MORETON-IN-MARSH, GL56 0AT
On A429 between Stratford-upon-Avon and Stow-on-the-Wold; tea shop at north end of main street, near station.
☕ Open daily; Tea served 10am-5pm Mon, 10am-4pm Tue, 10am-9.30pm Wed-Sat, 10.30am-9.30pm Sun

*B*lending with the numerous high-quality art and antiques shops in the High Street, The Marshmallow is a popular venue for tourists and locals alike. Tuesday is a particularly busy day, when the traders' market comes to this delightful Cotswold town. The tea shop is distinguished by its attractive frontage clad in colourful Virginia creeper; behind is a stone-flagged courtyard with tables and hanging baskets, where customers can take tea in the warmer months. The cake trolley is laden with tempting specialities including chocolate mousses, roulades, millefuille gateaux and pecan Danish pastries, all made on the premises.

The Tea Guild Award of Excellence 2004 .

RECOMMENDED IN THE AREA
Batsford Arboretum; Cotswold Falconry Centre; Sezincote house and garden

*T*wo Toads

Award-winning teashop with a lovely courtyard garden

☎ 01666 503696
✉ ken@twotoads.co.uk
🌐 www.twotoads.co.uk

Map ref 2 - ST89

19 Church Street, TETBURY, GL8 8JG
🍴 Open Mon-Sat 9am-5pm, Sun
10.30am-4.30pm; Tea served all day;
Closed 25, 26 Dec, 1 Jan; Booking
possible; Set tea price(s) £3.85-£5.50;
Seats 45 + 30 outside; No Smoking

A sunny yellow tea room dating from the 17th century, run by owners Ken and Peta who gave up busy careers to breathe life into this old place. The light, fresh interior is heightened by pale ash bentwood furniture, flowers and pretty prints, while music from the 1920s and 30s creates a relaxed mood. At the rear of the building, a lovely courtyard garden is popular on warm days, when large umbrellas offer shade from the sun. But indoors or out, the food is an equally tasty choice of baguettes, pasties, quiches and jacket potatoes, with clotted cream teas and 17 blends to decide between.

RECOMMENDED IN THE AREA

Chavenage House; Westonbirt Arboretum; Uley Tumulus

Greater London

Sheraton Skyline Hotel & Conference Centre ★★★★

A smart airport hotel within easy reach of all terminals

☎ 020 8759 2535
Ⓕ 020 8750 9150
Ⓔ res268_skyline@
  sheraton.com
Ⓦ www.sheraton.com/skyline

Map ref 3 - TQ18

Bath Road, HAYES, UB3 5BP
*M4 junct 4 for Heathrow, follow
Terminal 1,2 & 3 signs. Before airport
entrance take slip road to left for
0.25m signed A4 Central London.*
☕ Open daily; Tea served all day;
Set tea price(s) £13.50; Seats 85;
Parking 320
🛏 350 Rooms; S £89-£216,
D £89-£216

*P*ublic areas are light, spacious and extensive at this large, contemporary-style hotel close to Heathrow Airport. Facilities extend to a choice of restaurants, business centre, fitness centre, 18 meeting rooms, Sports Bar and Café, and the Perpetual Patisserie. 'Afternoon tea' is available all day in the tropical Sky Bar and Garden, or Bytes @ Sage, where snacks and light meals are served to eat in or take away. The set afternoon tea includes assorted finger sandwiches, fresh scones with clotted cream and jam, French pastries and a choice of teas. Dogs are permitted, and parking for over 300 cars is provided.

RECOMMENDED IN THE AREA
Windsor Castle; Hampton Court Palace; Legoland

70

Hampshire

The coming of the railways boosted sales of two crops in Hampshire that had traditionally been grown for local consumption. The first is strawberries, that began to be delivered bright and early to London on the 'Strawberry Specials' in the 1850s, and the second is watercress from the Alresford area. Hampshire is still the major supplier of watercress in the UK, a crop grown very specifically in shallow but fast moving water. Watercress is immensely popular these days, not only because its peppery leaves go down well in soup, salads and sandwiches, but because it is believed to have powerful medicinal properties.

Hampshire is also a great honey-producing area with a range that includes aromatic heather honey from the New Forest. Another treat from the New Forest are fabulous wild mushrooms.

*T*ylney Hall Hotel ★★★★ ◉◉

A Victorian country house set in extensive parkland

☎ 01256 764881
🖷 01256 768141
✉ sales@tylneyhall.com
Ⓦ www.tylneyhall.com

Map ref 3 - SU65

ROTHERWICK, RG27 9AZ
M3 junct 5, A287 to Basingstoke, over junct with A30, over railway bridge, towards Newnham. Right at Newnham Green. Hotel 1m on left.
☕ Open daily; Tea served 3.30pm-5.30pm daily; Booking required; Set tea price(s) £12.50; Seats 114 + 41 outside; Parking 120
🛏 112 Rooms; S £135-£400, D £165-£430

Tylney Hall is a superb Grade II listed property with impressive public rooms. Afternoon tea and light meals are served in the Italian Lounge by the log fire in winter or out on the garden terrace in summer. The fabulous grounds – some 66 acres – feature restored water gardens originally laid out by Gertrude Jekyll. On Saturday and Sunday the full Tylney Hall Tea may also include Welsh rarebit and a glass of champagne. Otherwise the set tea comprises a selection of sandwiches, home-made pastries, and scones with clotted cream and preserves. Reservations for tea are advisable for non-residents; parking available. Guide dogs only.

RECOMMENDED IN THE AREA
Winchester Cathedral; The Vyne; Stratfield Saye House

WALK

Hampshire - Rotherwick

A very pleasant short walk exploring the pretty countryside to the nort of Rotherwick. Along the way there are stretches of quiet woodland an good views over farmland to the south

With your back to Rotherwick church, turn left and pass Church Cottage. Walk through Rotherwick and on the left you'll see Whitewater primary school. Pass the Coach and Horses pub and continue through the village. On the right is an interesting map of the area and on the left is the Falcon pub. Turn left into Wedmans Lane and on the corner here is an old chapel which later became a funeral parlour. Disregard the turning to Lampards Close

and continue along the lane. Avoid the footpath at the entrance to October House and keep ahead for a few paces to a path crossing the lane. Turn left here and when you reach a sign prohibiting vans, bear left and follow an enclosed path to a footbridge and kissing gate. Keep right in the field and look for a stile in the boundary. Cross it and turn immediately left by some trees. At the waymark veer left into the adjacent field and then swing right,

keeping to the right edge. Make for the far right corner of the field where you'll find a gate and stile. Follow the boundary to another stile and turn left to follow the field edge. A large house looms into view just before you come to the road. Turn right here and pass a sign for Lyde Green. Turn left by the Fox pub and follow the lane as it bends left. Descend gently between trees and pass a gated track on the left Emerge from the woodland just before a house and turn sharp left in the field. Skirt the field for some time to reach a stile and waymark. Swing left here to two tracks. Take the left track and follow it to the road by the sign for Rotherwick. Cross over and keep on the track, passing a sign 'permissive path - walkers only'. Follow the track round to the right by barns and farm outbuildings and head for the road. Turn righ and return to the church.

DISTANCE: 2.75 miles/4.4km
START/FINISH: Rotherwick Church
MAP: OS Explorer 144
TERRAIN: Gently undulating countryside; country roads, paths and tracks
PATHS: Country roads, paths and tracks
GRADIENT: No steep hills

*T*he Montagu Arms Hotel ★★★ ✿✿

Historic hotel on the Beaulieu estate, with a character and charm that make visiting a delight

☎ 01590 612324 📠 01590 612188
✉ reservations@montaguarmshotel.co.uk
🌐 www.montaguarmshotel.co.uk

Map ref 3 - SU30

Palace Lane, BEAULIEU, SO42 7ZL *M27 junct 2, turn left at rdbt, follow signs for Beaulieu. Continue to Dibden Purlieu, then right at rdbt. Hotel on left.*
☕ Open daily; Tea served 3pm-6pm; Booking possible; Set tea price(s) £5.50;
Seats 30 + 45 outside; Parking 80; ⇿ 23 Rooms; S £100-£160, D £145-£210

RECOMMENDED IN THE AREA
National Motor Museum, Bucklers Hard, Exbury Gardens

Hospitality is top of the bill at this old world retreat, and its warmth extends equally to those resident in the hotel and those who stop by for refreshments. The 16th-century inn nestles in the pretty little hamlet of Beaulieu, where the National Motor Museum on the Beaulieu estate attracts many visitors. The historic shipbuilding village of Buckler's Hard is a short but pleasant walk away along the banks of the estuary, and the quaint High Street is worth a browse. On a cool day, the blazing log fires in the lounge encourage a relaxing doze on the comfortable sofas, and the conservatory with its outlook onto the terrace and gardens is another cosy spot. In both of these settings you can enjoy a traditional afternoon tea accompanied by a choice of speciality loose leaf teas like Russian Caravan. The charming staff bring finger sandwiches, loaf cakes, scones, cream tea fancies, shortbread, local jams, and strawberries. It's quintessential England at its best!

AA Courtesy & Care Award Winner for England 2003-4.

*D*e Vere
Grand Harbour ★★★★

A modern hotel sitting beside the old city walls

☎ 023 8063 3033
📠 023 8063 3066
✉ grandharbour@devere-hotels.com
🌐 www.deveregrandharbour.co.uk

Map ref 3 - SU41

West Quay Road, SOUTHAMPTON,
SO15 1AG
M27 junct 3 follow Waterfront signs, keep in left hand lane of dual carrriageway, then follow signs Heritage & Waterfront to old town & waterfront onto West Quay Rd.
☕ Open daily; Tea served 2.30pm-5.30pm; Credit cards accepted only if tea is paid for by phone (eg as a gift); Seats 75; No smoking areas; Air con; Parking 190;
🛏 172 Rooms; S £165-£195, D £185-£215

*S*outhampton's medieval walls and attractive waterfront are the location for this smart modern hotel, part of the respected De Vere Group. Visitors to the city, many of whom belong to the sailing fraternity, will find a warm welcome here, and a pleasant spot to while away a few hours over afternoon tea. The Turner's Bar is the setting for an extravaganza of scones, clotted cream, strawberry preserve, assorted sandwiches and pastries, served with a pot of your chosen tea. If you're feeling indulgent and shameless, you can add chocolate-covered strawberries and a glass of champagne to the menu above, and nod off for a while in the comfortable seating.

RECOMMENDED IN THE AREA
Tudor House; Maritime Museum; West Quay Shopping Centre

*G*ilbert White's House

Restored home of an early ecologist

☎ 01420 511275
✆ 01420 511040

Map ref 3 - SU72

The Wakes, SELBORNE, GU34 3JH
☕ Open daily; Tea served 11am-5pm;
Closed Christmas week; Booking possible
(except for weekends, special events and
BHs); Seats 24; No smoking

*T*he great naturalist himself would be familiar with the food served in this very English tea room, since it's all made from authentic 18th-century recipes. Produce from his garden goes into mushroom and chestnut pasty, homity pie, and tureen of hodge podge at lunchtime, and 'the best orange pudding that was ever tasted' dating from around 1714. A delicious array of cakes includes date and walnut slice, and the rich Rachel Manaton's plum cake, while a generous selection of speciality teas is freshly brewed to wash it all down. The tea parlour is furnished and decorated in period style, with original family paintings on the walls.

The Tea Guild Award of Excellence 2004.

RECOMMENDED IN THE AREA
Gilbert White's House & The Oates Museum; Jane Austen's House at Chawton; Bohunt Manor

---

*T*he Winchester Royal ★★★

Welcoming and friendly, an ideal venue for tea

☎ 01962 840840
✆ 01962 841582
✉ royal@marstonhotels.com
🌐 www.marstonhotels.com

Map ref 3 - SU42

Saint Peter Street, WINCHESTER,
SO23 8BS
M3 junct 9 to Winnal Trading Estate. Follow road to city centre, cross river, left, 1st right. Onto one-way system and 2nd right. Hotel immediately on right.
☕ Open daily; Tea served all day;
Set tea price(s) £9.50; Seats 40;
Parking 50
🛏 75 Rooms; S £99, D from £114

*Q*uietly tucked away down a side street but still in the heart of the historic city this former bishop's residence and convent (though not at the same time!). It dates in part from the 16th century, and has been a hotel for over 150 years. With its pleasant gardens and terrace it makes an ideal base for touring the city. One of its chief pleasures is the afternoon ritual of tea, served in the charming lounge throughout the day - no need to wait until 4pm. Expect scones, preserves, clotted cream, sandwiches and fruit cake, with a pot of tea to accompany.

RECOMMENDED IN THE AREA
Winchester Cathedral; Gurkha Museum; Hospital of St Cross

WALK

Hampshire - Selborne

A glorious woodland walk between the mighty beech trees of Selborne Hanger and then across delightful open country to tranquil Selborne Common

From the car park follow the path signed to Selborne Hanger, climbing the Zig Zag Path. With the view in front of you, swing left to some steps and then veer right at the fork in the clearing. Follow the well-used path through the woodland and stay on it as it gradually descends to reach a junction with a track. Turn right and follow the path between trees and hedgerows. Continue to the road and turn left. When the road bends sharp left, go straight on along a bridleway. After about 100 yards go through a gate on the left and head diagonally right across the pasture. Cross a track and maintain the same direction towards a tree in the next field. Make for a gate in the woodland and look for a bridleway waymark. Avoid a path on the left and continue on the bridleway as it runs to the right, narrowing to a path running between hedgerows and trees. Pass under pylon cables and take the path on the right to Farringdon. Descend a gentle slope, cross a stile and keep left at the road. Pass the Rose & Crown, then turn left opposite a house called Brownings Orchard. Follow the bridleway through the trees and when it bends right, cross several stiles, then go half left in the next field. Make for a path junction and go straight on across the fields. Turn left at the next stile and follow the field boundary towards woodland. Swing right at a footpath sign and follow a clear track. Keep left at the fork and continue all the way to the road. Turn right, then left at an octagonal lodge. Climb gently through the parkland of Newton Valence Place, cross a drive and follow the path across a field to pass beside a holly and laurel hedge. Keep to the left of the church and cross fields to a galvanised gate. Cross over to a waymark and follow the path signposted Selborne. Keep right at the fork, avoid a path on the right and cross a stile at the woodland corner. Walk ahead along the field edge and round to the left almost immediately. Make for a kissing gate and continue through two galvanised kissing gates. Go down the track and return to the car park.

DISTANCE: 7.25 miles/11.7km
START/FINISH: Selborne
MAP: OS Explorer 133
TERRAIN: Woodland, pasture and parkland
GRADIENT: The Zig Zag Path is the main climb on this walk

Speciality Teas:
• take their name from the plantation on which they are grown (usually referred to as single estate or single source teas)
• come from a particular area or country
• are blended for a particular time of day or occasion
• are blends to which flower, fruit, herb or spice flavourings have been added.

Taiwan, Japan and Sri Lanka

Taiwanese Teas
Formosa Oolong
When farmers from China's Fujian Province emigrated to the island of Formosa (now Taiwan) in the 1850s, they took with them their traditional methods of manufacturing tea. The best of Taiwan's oolongs are produced on the slopes of Mount Dung Ding. The infusion is orange-green and has a light, smooth taste. Drink without milk.

Japanese Teas
Sencha
This is the most common and popular of Japan's green teas. The freshly-picked leaves are first steamed and then fluffed by hot air and rolled, dried and polished to become flat, dark green, needle-like leaves. These brew quickly to give a pale yellow, very clear infusion that has a soft, herbal taste. No milk please.

Gyokuro
The very best of Japan's green teas requires special care and attention. The bushes are covered for about three weeks before being plucked, with canvas or reed mats to reduce the amount of light reaching the bushes as they grow. This means that the leaves produce more chlorophyll and have a much more concentrated sweet flavour than Sencha. Gyokuro is ground down to a fine powder to make 'matcha', which is then whisked into hot water and drunk during the famous Japanese Tea Ceremony. Drink without milk.

Teas from Sri Lanka (Ceylon)
Dimbula
Grown at 5,000 ft above sea level, Dimbula black teas a light, bright infusion and a crisp, strong flavour. Dimbula was one of the first areas of the island to be planted with tea after the demise of the coffee estates in the 1860s. Drink with or without milk.

Nuwara Eliya
Black teas from the hill country in the centre of the island are among Sri Lanka's finest. The even pieces of brown leaf give a rich golden liquor that has a lightly perfumed brisk flavour.

Uva
This fine flavoured black tea comes from the eastern slopes of the central mountains of Sri Lanka where the dry wind has a marked effect on the quality and character of the tea. Uva teas are bright in colour and have a dry, crisp taste. Enjoy with or without milk.

Herefordshire

Herefordshire has a strong history of apple growing and cider making. The industry probably peaked around 1877 when there were 22,000 acres of apple orchards in the county, compared to a century later when there were just 6,000 acres across Herefordshire and Worcestershire combined. Nevertheless, Herefordshire is still Big Apple Country with both apples and cider figuring prominently in local recipes, such as Hereford apple dumplings and cider cake. Tourists interested in the cider-making process might like to follow the Herefordshire Cider Trail, visiting a number of cider makers and sampling their products. Hereford beef is another prime product, renowned for its tenderness and flavour.

*M*rs Muffin's Teashop

Local produce and fine home cooking

☎ 01531 633579

Map ref 2 - SO63

1 Church Lane, LEDBURY, HR8 1DL
☕ Open 10am-5pm; Tea served all day; Closed 24 Dec-mid Jan; Booking possible; No credit cards; Seats 36; No Smoking; No Dogs

*T*hese award-winning tea rooms in the attractive Herefordshire town of Ledbury are set in an area noted for its hop-growing. Visitors enjoying this rural part of the country will relish the pretty gardens at Mrs Muffin's in the summer, while the cosy interior comes into its own at any time of year. The menu is notable for its use of local produce, such as apple juice, cheese and ice cream. Look out for the home-made soups, toasted sandwiches and jacket potatoes, and indulge yourself with some wonderful home-baked cakes, served with properly-made tea. Jams, chutneys and apple juice are also on sale, along with recipe books.

The Tea Guild Award of Excellence 2004.

RECOMMENDED IN THE AREA
Eastnor Castle; Hereford Cathedral; Cider Museum & King Offa Distillery

Hertfordshire

Hertfordshire was the home of the malting industry from the 1700s till the 1900s, based on its abundant barley harvest. At one time the county had 44 breweries, but only one of these still remains, McMullen and Sons, which has been brewing beer in Hertford for over 170 years. These days, Hertfordshire is a largely urban county, accommodating the spread from London. The first of Britain's planned cities were built here, Letchworth and then Welwyn Garden City. There are no well-known delicacies associated with the county, but do look out for locally made goats' cheeses, including the Hertfordshire Speckle, made in St Albans by Elizabeth and David Harris.

Sopwell House Hotel ★★★★ ◈◉

A Georgian country house set in 12 acres of gardens

☎ 01727 864477
🅕 01727 844741/845636
🅔 enquiries@
   sopwellhouse.co.uk
🅦 www.sopwellhouse.co.uk

Map ref 3 - TL10

Cottonmill Lane, Sopwell,
ST ALBANS, AL1 2HQ
*M25 junct 22, follow A1081 St Albans.
At 3rd lights, turn left into Mill House
Lane, over mini rdbt into Cottonmill
Lane.*
☕ Open daily; Tea served daily;
Booking required; Set tea price(s)
£14.50; Seats 180 inc patio area;
No smoking areas; Parking 350;
🛏 129 Rooms; S £99-£129,
D £158-£169

An imposing property in a secluded setting amid its own grounds, this is a large hotel with an exclusive ambience and particularly impressive leisure facilities. Afternoon tea is available in the Brasserie restaurant, terrace bar, library or patio. Fresh leaf and fruit teas are served and cakes can be ordered individually. A set Traditional Afternoon Tea is offered, comprising finger sandwiches, fruit and plain scones with preserves and Devonshire clotted cream, pastries and tea or coffee. For an extra special treat there is the set Champagne Afternoon Tea. Ample parking is provided; no dogs.

RECOMMENDED IN THE AREA
*St Alban's Cathedral; Garden of the Rose;
Verulanium Museum*

Kent

Kent is at the heart of the south-east England fruit growing area and is well known for its apples and cherries. Fruit pies, puddings and turnovers are clear favourites with all that wonderful produce around, but there are some recipes peculiar to the area, such as cherry bumpers (a kind of turnover). Kentish huffkins are flat oval loaves of bread with a soft crust and a deep indentation at the centre, and oast cakes are balls of dough fried in lard, traditionally taken by hop pickers out into the fields to keep them going during the day.

Kent Lent pie, also known as Kentish pudding pie, is a short pastry case filled with a mixture of butter, sugar, eggs, cream and ground rice cooked with milk.

Eastwell Manor ★★★★ ◉◉

An English custom in a historic country hotel

☎ 01233 213000
📠 01233 635530
✉ eastwell@btinternet.com
🌐 www.eastwellmanor.co.uk

Map ref 4 - TR03

Eastwell Park, Boughton Lees, ASHFORD, TN25 4HR
M20 Junct 9 on A251, 200yds on left when entering Boughton Aluph.
☕ Open daily; Tea served 2.30pm-5.30pm; Booking required; Set tea price(s) £8.00, £13.00, £18.50; Seats 50; Parking 200;
🛏 62 Rooms; S £170, D £200

Warming log fires, leather armchairs, discreet and friendly service – few places are more conducive to relaxing over afternoon tea. In summer the 60 acres of grounds surrounding this historic house lend themselves to sipping Earl Grey or another of the 22 varieties of speciality teas. Indoors or out, there is little to beat the splendid setting. The afternoon tea menu is equally impressive: try the Traditional Cream or Eastwell Manor teas, or to really push the boat out, the Champagne tea. sandwiches, cakes and scones with clotte cream and jam are not enough to satisf you can add muffins and crumpets.

RECOMMENDED IN THE AREA
Leeds Castle; Sissinghurst Gardens; Canterbury Cathedral

*C*laris's

A quintessentially English tea shop with beams, inglenook, lace tablecloths, and delicious food

☎ 01580 291025
✉ info@collectablegifts.net
🌐 www.collectablegifts.net

Map ref 4 - TQ84

1-3 High Street, BIDDENDEN,
TN27 8AL
From M20 J8, take B2163 South, L onto A274 to Biddenden. From J9, take A28 South, R onto A262 to Biddenden. From J5, take A21 South, L onto A262 to Biddenden.
🍵 Open 10.30-5.20; Tea served all day; Closed Mon, early Jan-early Feb; Set tea price(s) £3.85; No credit cards; Seats 24 + 16 outside; No Smoking

A 15th-century weaver's cottage in one of England's most unspoilt villages is the setting for a flourishing tea room and gift shop. Collectors of such diverse objects as fine pottery and Steiff teddy bears are drawn to this Aladdin's cave of treasures, found in the half-timbered High Street of what was once the centre of the cloth trade. Behind the windows filled temptingly with Moorcroft pottery, lamps, glassware, enamels and soft toys, the tea shop itself exudes charm. The low oak beams and inglenook fireplace, and spacious tables covered in lace, are outdone in appeal only by the delicious food served here. Huge light meringues are a house speciality, but equally irresistible are the wonderful walnut bread, lemon Madeira, almond slice and coffee walnut cake. Cream teas come with a rich choice of brews, and there are also soups and sandwiches, or snacks such as creamed mushrooms on toast. Janet and Brian Wingham are thoughtful and welcoming hosts, and their obvious love of their tea shop is contagious.

The Tea Guild Award of Excellence 2004.

RECOMMENDED IN THE AREA

Biddenden Vineyards & Cider Works; Sissinghurst Castle Garden; Smallhythe Place

WALK

Across Romney Marshes

An atmospheric walk across moody marshlands.

In The Ingoldsby Legends (1837) Revd Richard Barham declared that the world: 'is divided into Europe, Asia, Africa, America and Romney Marsh'. The name is thought to derive from the Saxon 'Rumnea' meaning marsh water.

This walk takes you between two historic marsh villages, starting at Ivychurch. Park by the Bell Inn, next to St George's Church, built in the 1360s. During the Civil War, Cromwell's soldiers slept here and even stabled their horses in the church. Inside the church you can see some stone seats along one wall. These were reserved for the elderly, in the days before churches had pews. It's one explanation for the saying: 'let the weakest go to the wall'.

With the church on your left, walk along the road, pass the phone box, then take the footpath on the right. Go diagonally left across this field keeping the mast on your right. Walk around the edge of the next field, cross over a bridge and continue until you reach Yoakes Lane. At the lane, turn right and follow it all the way to Old Romney. At Old Romney you come to the busy main road (A259), turn left here and walk down, before turning left again. Take time to stop in Old Romney and visit the church before continuing the walk. It's set back from the road and dates back to the 11th or 12th century.

There is now a choice of routes. You can follow Five Vents Lane all the way back to Ivychurch, or go up the lane, walk around a curved medieval moat and follow the ditch, walking around the field edges and crossing two bridges, to arrive back at Yoakes Lane. You can retrace your steps to reach the village, or turn right and continue along Yoakes Lane to the main road. When you reach the road, turn left and walk back to the Bell Inn and your starting point.

WHAT TO LOOK FOR

In spring you might well hear a raucous croaking noise rising from the ditches in the marsh. It's the sound of the marsh frog, known locally as the 'laughing frog'. Twelve were introduced to a garden pond in 1935 and soon escaped into the surrounding marshland

DISTANCE: 3 miles (4.8km)
START/FINISH: The Bell Inn, Ivychurch
MAP: OS Explorer 125
TERRAIN : Field edges and lanes- can be muddy
GRADIENT: Level

*T*he Hythe Imperial ★★★★ ◉

Grand old hotel serving tea with a view

☎ 01303 267441
🖷 01303 264610
✉ hytheimperial@
   marstonhotels.com
🌐 www.marstonhotels.com

Map ref 4 - TR13

Princes Parade, HYTHE, CT21 6AE
M20, junct 11 onto A261. In Hythe follow Folkestone signs. Right into Twiss Rd to hotel.
☕ Open daily; Tea served 3pm-5.30pm; Closed 25-Dec; Booking possible; Set tea price(s) £9.50; Seats 60; Smoking allowed in certain areas; No dogs; Parking 200;
🛏 100 Rooms; S £108, D £158

*M*ajestically set right on the seafront and surrounded by 50 acres of grounds, this impressive hotel dates from Victorian times. A thorough makeover has brought facilities and services up to a 21st-century standard, but the elegance and style of a much earlier age remain indelibly stamped on its fabric. Views of the sea, private golf course and gardens can be enjoyed from many of the rooms, and there are fabulous leisure facilities for staying guests. Tea is a constant afternoon factor, enjoyed in one of the upstairs lounges (more views), or in the Terrace Bar. Expect the delicious 'usual suspects', and a choice of teas.

RECOMMENDED IN THE AREA

Romney; Hythe & Dymchurch Railway; Port Lympne Zoo; Dover Castle

*C*hilston Park Hotel ★★★★ ◉◉

Comfort, warmth and peace – and afternoon tea

☎ 01622 859803
🖷 01622 858588
✉ chilstonpark@handpicked.co.uk
🌐 www.handpicked.co.uk/
   chilstonpark

Map ref 4 - TQ85

Sandway, LENHAM, ME17 2BE
from A20 into Lenham village, turn right onto High St, pass railway station on right, 1st left, over crossroads, hotel 0.25 mile on left.
☕ Open daily; Tea served 3pm-5pm; Booking required; Set tea price(s) £7.50, £12.50; Seats 60; Parking 100;
🛏 53 Rooms; S £90-£140, D £90-£295

*E*scape from the bustle of modern life by stealing a few hours in this calm oasis. The elegant 17th-century country house is steeped in tradition, its staff trained to uphold the values of an earlier age when service was unquestioningly offered. This motif still runs through the hotel, and nowhere more so than in the Drawing Room where afternoon tea is served in front of an open fire. Surrounded by paintings and antiques, you can enjoy fittingly fine teas with scones, strawberry jam and clotted cream, or the same plus finger sandwiches, pastries and cakes. On warm summer afternoons the terrace and gardens are even more delightful settings.

RECOMMENDED IN THE AREA

Leeds Castle; Canterbury; Bluewater Shopping Centre

83

Lancashire

Lancashire has a reputation for no-nonsense food, like tripe and onions, black pudding and cow heel pie, none of them for the faint hearted, but for tea what could be more refined than potted Morecambe Bay shrimps? Other regional favourites include old wives' sod, a dish of baked eggs and toasted oatcakes; Manchester tart, a pastry case spread with jam, sprinkled with dessicated coconut and topped with custard; and Manchester pudding, which is really also a tart filled with a breadcrumb, egg and milk mixture flavoured with brandy. Wet Nelly (actually from Liverpool), is a surprisingly popular concoction of pastry, cake or biscuit scraps soaked in syrup, the best bit being at the bottom where the syrup settles. Eccles Cakes and Chorley cakes are perhaps the most widely known of the Lancashire delicacies, both similar in presentation and content – large round pastries crammed with currants.

Café Caprice

Home-made cakes, gingerbreads and parkins, and friendly service

☏ 01200 422034

✉ cafecaprice@talk21.com

Map ref 6 - SD74

6-8 Moor Lane, CLITHEROE, BB7 1BE

🍵 Open Tue, Thu, Fri 9.30am-4.30pm; Sat 9am-4.30pm; Tea served all day; Closed Sun, Mon, Wed; Set tea price(s) £2.60; No credit cards; Seats 53

RECOMMENDED IN THE AREA
Clitheroe Castle Museum; Gawthorpe Hall; Samlesbury Hall

Vibrant colours on the walls, in the tablecloths and in the outfits worn by the staff suggest a wholly modern outlook at this popular Lancashire café. But appearances can be deceptive, and the traditional approach to the food and old-fashioned hospitality are as firmly in place as ever. The teatime menu features a stunning range of goodies, including Cumbrian lemon loaf, carrot cake, orange Victoria sandwich and lime and coconut slice. Parkins and gingerbreads are a house speciality, and particular teas are recommended to go with each one. The ever-popular scones with strawberry jam and cream still have pride of place, though, especially around 4pm.

The Tea Guild Award of Excellence 2004.

*T*oby Jug Tea Shop

Richly atmospheric tea shop in a conservation area

☎ / 🖷 01254 823298

Map ref 6 - SD74

20 King Street, CLITHEROE, BB7 9SL
🍵 Open Thu-Sat 10.30am-4.30pm;
Tea served all day; Closed 2 weeks at
Christmas, 2 weeks at end June; No
credit cards; Seats 30; No Smoking

The rich history behind this listed building partly explains the very special atmosphere which always strikes visitors. One of the oldest in the conservation village of Whalley, it is bordered by a 14th-century mill-race and sits on a once-important pilgrim's route. Oak beams and panelling plundered from the nearby Cistercian abbey add to its charm. The Ireland family opened the tea shop in 1985, since when it has gained an enviable reputation as a traditional English Tea Shop. The lunch menu includes an imaginative selection of sandwiches, salads and delicious seasonal soups. There is always an array of tempting cakes, scones and fruit pies, all prepared in the family kitchen, your choice will be complimented by one of the many teas or coffees offered from the extensive range.

RECOMMENDED IN THE AREA

Clitheroe Castle Museum; Gawthorpe Hall; Whitaker Park & Rossendale Museum

A TEA TO SUIT YOUR WATER

Next time you're enjoying a cup of tea, whether it be in your own home or in one of the tea rooms in this guide, spare a thought for the farmers, growers, buyers, and blenders throughout the world who worked to bring your tea to our shores.

Keith Writer, Tea Buyer for family tea merchants Taylors of Harrogate, is one such man. Keith's job takes him to the

Keith Writer, Tea Buyer at Taylors of Harrogate.

world's best tea estates and gardens on a quest to find teas to use in his Yorkshire Tea blend. He carefully assesses each and every tea he comes across to see if it will make the grade. Only those that give the perfect balance of strength, colour, flavour, and character are chosen. Meeting the growers is also important and gives Keith the opportunity to find out about working and living conditions on the estates. According to Keith, "Our philosophy is simple – to build long-term partnerships with people who are interested in growing good quality tea and running well-managed estates."

Tea in India, ready for plucking.

Keith presents an estate in Assam with a Yorkshire Tea Quality award.

Keith's dedication to bringing you a great cup of tea doesn't end there. As the business's third – generation Tea Buyer, Keith stands by the traditional craft of blending tea to suit the water. Back in Victorian times, tea merchants would test tea after tea to find the ones that performed best using the local water. That attention to detail has all but disappeared, expect in a handful of independent tea merchants. Keith and his small

Each tea is carefully tasted.

team collect water samples from all over the country. Then they blend Yorkshire Tea for Hard Water and a traditional Yorkshire Tea blend for areas with soft or medium water.

If you'd like a water testing kit to find out if you have hard water, or if you'd like a sample of either blend of Yorkshire Tea to try, just contact Taylors of Harrogate on 0500 418898.

Traditional tea caddies at Bettys.

A piece of tea history – the final lot of tea from the last London Tea Auction, bought by Taylors.

London

London's Chelsea buns date back to the 17th century, when they were made in prodigious quantities, many thousands a day, by Captain Bun (aka Richard Hand) at The Old Chelsea Bun House on Pimlico Road. The good captain was renowned for his eccentric business attire – a dressing gown and fez. The patronage of George III, who parked his carriage outside the shop, helped secure its phenomenal success. Though the shop was destroyed in the 19th century, the popularity of the delicious sticky buns is undiminished today. Chelsea buns are made by spreading a sheet of sweet yeast dough with dried fruit and rolling it up and cutting it into slices to form a bun in cross section.

Cockney culture in London's East End has its own traditional foods, such as oysters, fried fish (the precurser of fish and chips), pie and mash and perhaps the most unprepossessing of all delicacies – jellied eels. It is clear from the old nursery rhyme, 'Have you seen the muffin man, the muffin man, the muffin man, have you seen the muffin man who lives in Drury Lane' that muffins were traditionally sold on the streets of London apparently up until the 1930s. These would have been English muffins, made from a yeast-raised dough cooked in flat rounds on a griddle, and still sold as tea breads today. The English muffin should not to be confused with the American muffin, generally available in the UK these days, which is more like a cup cake in appearance.

*A*thenaeum Hotel & Apartments ★★★★★ ◉

A hospitable hotel with warm, stylish reception rooms

☎ 020 7499 3464
🖷 020 7493 1860
✉ info@athenaeumhotel.com
🌐 www.athenaeumhotel.com

Map ref 3 - TQ37

116 Piccadilly, LONDON, W1J 7BJ
on Piccadilly, overlooking Green Park.
♟ Open daily; Tea served 3pm-6pm;
Booking required; Set tea price(s)
£10.50, £17.00, £19.50;
Seats 25; Air con
🛏 157 Rooms; S £265-£600,
D £285-£750

The Athenaeum is one of London's leading independent five star hotels famed for offering discreet and personalised service. One of its most sought after retreats is the Windsor Lounge, a blissfully secluded room where friends can meet as if at home. Afternoons in the lounge are devoted to taking tea and a special menu presents some enticing choices. The Windsor is a straightforward yet mouth-watering affair of scones, clotted cream, preserves and traditional teas. Move up a notch for the grander Palace Tea, when sandwiches and pastries join the scones, or yet higher for a glass of champagne with the Athenaeum Royal Tea.

RECOMMENDED IN THE AREA
Buckingham Palace; Royal Academy of Arts; Kensington Gardens

---

*T*he Bentley Hotel ★★★★★

Choice of de-luxe teas in opulent surroundings

☎ 020 7244 5555
🖷 020 7244 5566
✉ info@thebentley-hotel.com
🌐 www.thebentley-hotel.com

Map ref 3 - TQ37

27-33 Harrington Gardens, LONDON,
SW7 4JX
directly S of A4 leading into Knightsbridge at the junct with Gloucester Rd.
♟ Open daily; Tea served 3pm-6pm;
Booking required; Set tea price(s)
£21.00, £25.00, £30.00; No credit
cards; Seats 50; Air con; 64 Rooms;
S £293.75, D £499.37

A luxury new hotel occupying a white-fronted terraced building in South Kensington, just off the busy Gloucester Road. The sumptuous interior is lined with marble, and in keeping with such grandeur, guest comfort has not been spared. A full-sized Turkish hammam, Jacuzzi baths, and a signature restaurant are among the delights waiting to be sampled. Afternoon tea is another pleasure in store for visitors to the hotel lounge, where nearly 20 teas and ten coffees can be ordered with or without cakes and pastries. For the Bentley tea, the Chocolate Afternoon tea, or the Champagne tea, expect a selection of outstanding delicacies.

RECOMMENDED IN THE AREA
Royal Albert Hall; Victoria & Albert Museum; Earls Court

*T*he Berners Hotel ★★★★

A traditional-style hotel in London's West End

☎ 020 7666 2000
🖷 020 7666 2001
✉ berners@berners.co.uk
🌐 www.thebernershotel.co.uk

Map ref 3 - TQ37

Berners Street, LONDON, W1A 3BE
☕ Open daily; Tea served 3pm-
5.30pm daily; Booking required;
Set tea price(s) £11.95; Seats 40 + 25
in bar
🛏 216 Rooms; S £190, D £215

*B*erners Hotel is an elegant early 20th-century conversion of five classic town houses dating from 1835, located just off Oxford Street. The hotel's sumptuous lobby, with its elaborately carved Grade II listed ceiling, is a popular rendezvous for morning coffee and afternoon tea – the perfect retreat during a West End shopping expedition. The set afternoon tea includes a selection of freshly-cut finger sandwiches, smoked salmon and cream cheese bagels, delicious pastries and a home-made scone with jam and clotted cream, accompanied by your choice from a range of teas or an assortment of fruit infusions. Guide dogs only.

RECOMMENDED IN THE AREA
Oxford Street; West End Theatres; Covent Garden

---

*T*he Carlton Tower Hotel ★★★★★ ◉◉

Superior teas accompanied by a harpist

☎ 020 7235 1234
🖷 020 7235 9129
✉ contact@carltontower.com
🌐 www.carltontower.com

Map ref 3 - TQ37

Cadogan Place, LONDON, SW1X 9PY
*A4 towards Knightsbridge, turn right onto
Sloane St. Hotel on left before Cadogan Pl.*
☕ Open daily; Tea served 3pm-6pm;
Booking possible; Set tea price(s) £22.50,
£27.50; Seats 70; Air con
🛏 220 Rooms; S £234-£382, D £234-£382

*I*n the glamorous Chinoiserie lounge they serve summer drinks and exotic juices, spirits and wines, club sandwiches and desserts, but perhaps nothing has quite the appeal of the 'nice cup of tea'. To the soothing sound of a harpist playing gently in the background, devotees of the classic afternoon repast can choose between the Carlton Tower and the Knightsbridge, depending on their taste for champagne and strawberries. With or without these exotic extras, you can expect assorted sandwiches, plain and raisin scones served with Devonshire clotted cream and daringly untraditional tayberry and apricot jams, plus a selection of French pastries. Still hungry? They serve salads and light meals til very late.

RECOMMENDED IN THE AREA
Hyde Park; London Eye; Harrods

WALK

London - The City

Follow this trail to the heart of the City of London, a fascinating blend of ancient and modern

From The Monument walk along Monument Street and as you approach the junction with Lower Thames Street, turn left into cobbled Lovat Lane. Pass The Walrus and the Carpenter pub and look for the church of St Mary at Hill - Billingsgate's parish church. Visit the church, leave by a different exit and turn left to the junction with Eastcheap. Turn right into Great Tower Street and as you approach All Hallows Church, cross over into Mark Lane, then right into Hart Street. Pass Seething Lane and continue into Crutched Friars. Walk beneath the railway and turn left into Lloyds Avenue.

Turn right along Fenchurch Street towards St Botulph's Church, Aldgate. Keep left here and take Dukes Place, following it along to Camomile Street. Cross Bishopsgate and pass All Hallows London Wall Church. Cross Broad Street and turn left into Copthall Avenue. When the road bends left, veer right towards Copthall Buildings and head for Telegraph Street. Turn left at Moorgate and walk along to the back of the Bank of England. Turn right here and follow Gresham Street to Guildhall Yard. Pass St Lawrence Jewry, the church of the Corporation of London, and turn left into Milk Street. Turn right on reaching Cheapside and walk along to St Paul's Cathedral. Retrace your steps briefly along Cheapside and look for an arch on the right. Once

through the arch, turn immediately left to some steps and cross Broad Street to a passage which leads to St Mary-le-Bow. Keep to the right of the church, turn right at the junction and walk along the narrow pedestrianised street for a few paces, turning left into Well Court. Follow it round to the right, cross Queen Street into Pancras Lane, then cross Queen Victoria Street to Bucklersbury. Keep to the left of the Saxon church of St Stephen Walbrook and follow the alleyway, St Stephen's Row, alongside it. Look for the little churchyard, hemmed in by buildings, and turn right at the next junction. Turn left into St St Swithin's Lane and walk along to the Bank of England and the Royal Exchange. Look for the signs for the tube station.

DISTANCE: 3 miles/4.8km
START : The Monument
FINISH: Bank tube station
MAP: AA Street by Street London
TERRAIN : Pavements, streets and alleyways
GRADIENT: Level

*T*he Dorchester ★★★★

A time-honoured afternoon institution in the palatial surroundings of this London landmark

☎ 020 7629 8888 📠 020 7317 6464
✉ foodandbeverage@dorchesterhotel.com
🌐 www.dorchesterhotel.com

Map ref 3 - TQ37

Park Lane, LONDON, W1A 2HJ
(halfway along Park Lane between Hyde Park Corner & Marble Arch).
♟ Open 6am-1am; Tea served 2.30pm-6pm daily; Booking required;
Set tea price(s) £28.50, £34.50, £38.50; Seats 100; Guide dogs only;
🛏; 240 Rooms; S £317-£370.13, D £387.75-£452.38

RECOMMENDED IN THE AREA
Petrie Museum of Egyptian Archaeology; National Portrait Gallery; Museum of the Royal College of Surgeons

*T*aking afternoon tea at The Dorchester - the phrase conjures up sumptuous images of well-mannered staff, beautifully-prepared delicacies and fragile bone china. Even such vaulted expectations are likely to be exceeded at this byword for hospitality, with its marble pillars, magnificent flower arrangements, amazingly comfortable sofas and armchairs, and air of refinement. The staff are well-trained, but they are friendly too, and visitors are quickly put at their ease and made to feel at home. In the Promenade you can sample finger sandwiches, scones with clotted cream and jam, and fresh pastries made by the restaurants patissier, all served with a speciality tea such as China Oolong, Russian Caravan, or the Dorchester's own house blend (or glass of champagne for special occasions). Second and third helpings are always offered, but it's a rare customer who can last the full course. When it comes to five-star teas in a suitably opulent setting, this one is hard to beat.

Winner of The Tea Guild's Top London Afternoon Tea Award 2002.

*T*he Chesterfield ★★★★ ◉

Enjoy a satisfying tea in an atmosphere of charm & character

☎ 020 7491 2622
🖷 020 7491 4793
✉ bookch@rchmail.com
🌐 www.chesterfieldmayfair.com

Map ref 3 - TQ37

35 Charles Street, Mayfair, LONDON, W1J 5EB
From Hyde Park corner along Piccadilly, left into Half Moon St. At end left and 1st right into Queens St, then right into Charles St.
☕ Tea served 3pm-5.30pm daily; Set tea price(s) from £7.95; Seats 20; Air con
🛏 110 Rooms; S £145-£195, D £155-£225

Smartly located in the heart of Mayfair, this hotel was once the home of the Earl of Chesterfield, and it still retains the charm and character of a bygone era. Its clublike atmosphere is emphasised by wood panelling, oil paintings and leather armchairs, and in these august surroundings, the afternoon tea is perfectly at home. The more adventurous may go for the Champagne Tea, a snip at £19.50, while traditionalists will be drawn to the Devonshire Cream Tea, or the Chesterfield, a mini-banquet of sandwiches, scones with clotted cream, pastries and éclairs, and various cakes. The choice of special teas includes Darjeeling and Ceylon.

RECOMMENDED IN THE AREA
Buckingham Palace; Hyde Park; Bond Street

---

*I*nterContinental The Churchill London ★★★★★ ◉◉◉

A classic venue for an essentially English meal

☎ 020 7486 5800
🖷 020 7486 1255
✉ churchill@interconti.com
🌐 www.london-churchill.intercontinental.com

Map ref 3 - TQ37

30 Portman Square, LONDON, W1A 4ZX
From Marble Arch rdbt, follow signs for Oxford Circus onto Oxford St. Left turn after 2nd lights onto Portman St. Hotel on left.
☕ Tea served 3pm-6pm daily; Booking required; Set tea price(s) fr £9.50; Seats 140; Air con; Parking 48;
🛏 445 Rooms; S £320, D £320

A menu listing a staggering 70-plus different kinds of teas is a sure indication of how seriously the afternoon ritual is taken here. The glitzy Terrace on Portman Square features indoor trees and bright chandeliers, the perfect place for enjoying what was seen in the 19th century as 'the ideal way to break up the lengthy interval between luncheon and dinner'. The Churchill version varies between the modest Blenheim cream tea, the more challenging Terrace Tiffin – think cream tea plus a selection of finger sandwiches, French pastries and fruit tartlets – and the unspeakably luxurious Champagne High Tea, incorporating all of the Tiffin plus scrambled eggs and caviar, and champagne.

RECOMMENDED IN THE AREA
Hyde Park; Bond Street & Oxford Street shops; Madame Tussauds

93

*F*our Seasons Hotel London ★★★★★ ◉◉

A hospitable hotel with an exclusive address, and quality teas to match

☎ 020 7499 0888
🖷 020 7493 1895
✉ fsh.london@fourseasons.com
🌐 www.fourseasons.com

Map ref 3 - TQ37

Hamilton Place, Park Lane, LONDON,
W1A 1AZ
*From Piccadilly into Old Park Lane, then
Hamilton Place.*
🍽 Open 8am-10pm; Tea served 3pm-7pm
daily; Booking possible; Set tea price(s)
£23, £32.50; Seats 60; No smoking areas;
Air con
🛏 220 Rooms; S £305-£1500,
D £360-£2200

With more than 60 varieties of tea on the menu, it is hardly surprising that Four Seasons Hotel London received The Tea Council's 2003 award for Best Tea Place in London. The amazing choice, including their own Four Seasons Anniversary blend, is not the only reason for this recognition however. The elegant surroundings of the Lounge, the tinkling of a piano in the background, and the delicate china bearing sandwiches, warm scones with clotted cream and jam, and some irresistible French pastries all contribute to an unforgettable experience. The champagne tea is an extra indulgence, and even latecomers won't miss out because servings go on until 7pm. Light meals and snacks are also available in the Lounge throughout the day, with a pre-theatre menu for early diners. This smart hotel, located in the stylish area of Park Lane, is particularly well-known for its hospitality and service.

Winner of The Tea Guild's Top London Afternoon Tea Award 2003.

RECOMMENDED IN THE AREA
Buckingham Palace; Royal Academy of Arts; Hyde Park

*T*he Goring ★★★★★ ◉◉

highlight of a visit or stay – the Goring Tea

☎ 020 7396 9000
🖷 020 7834 4393
✉ reception@goringhotel.co.uk
🌐 www.goringhotel.co.uk

Map ref 3 - TQ37

Beeston Place, Grosvenor Gardens, LONDON, SW1W 0JW
off Lower Grosvenor Place, just before Royal Mews.
☕ Tea served 3.30pm-5pm daily; Set tea price(s) £15.00; Seats 50; Air con; No Dogs; Parking 7;
🛏 74 Rooms; S £200-£450, D £230-£450

Ever since the Goring opened its doors in 1910, afternoon tea has been a constant feature. This icon of hospitality serves its classic set tea in the comfort of various reception rooms including the Lounge and the Terrace. The menu is long, and probably best enjoyed in the company of friends gathered for an enjoyable chat; start with a selection of sandwiches, move on to home-made scones with clotted cream and jam, then try some of the traditional pastries – don't forget to keep a little space for the Goring fruit cake, or a portion of sachertorte with Chantilly cream. Several speciality teas and the house blend will accompany this feast.

RECOMMENDED IN THE AREA
Queen's Gallery, Royal Mews; Westminster Abbey

*I*nterContinental London ★★★★★ ◉◉

Enjoy a range of luxury teas in smart surroundings

☎ 020 7409 3131
🖷 020 7493 3476
✉ london@interconti.com
🌐 www.london.intercontinental.com

Map ref 3 - TQ37

Hamilton Place, Hyde Park Corner, LONDON, W1J 7QY
At Hyde Park Corner, on corner of Park Ln and Piccadilly.
☕ Tea served 3pm-6pm; Closed Sat; Booking required; Set tea price(s) fr £9.50; Seats 40; Air con; Guide dogs only
🛏 451 Rooms; S £320, D £320

Lovers of that great British institution, afternoon tea, would be hard-pressed to find a better exponent of the famous ritual than this landmark London hotel. Between the hours of 3 and 6pm, tea drinkers can betake themselves to the stylish lounge and indulge in the Mayfair Tea – the height of luxury with a glass of champagne, smoked salmon sandwiches, French pastries, scones with clotted cream and jam, and a pot of tea of your choice. The Hyde Park Tea, the Parisian Tea and the Devonshire Tea are only slightly less extravagant, and there are several choices of coffee available for those who like to be different!

RECOMMENDED IN THE AREA
Buckingham Palace; Hyde Park; Royal Albert Hall

*T*he Lanesborough ★★★★★ ⊚⊚

Delicious teas made using revived Russian methods

☏ 020 7259 5599
🖷 020 7259 5606
✉ info@lanesborough.co.uk
🌐 www.lanesborough.com

Map ref 3 - TQ37

Hyde Park Corner, LONDON,
SW1X 7TA
*Follow signs to central London and
Hyde Park Corner.*
🍵 Tea served 3.30pm-6pm daily;
Booking possible; Set tea price(s) fr
£24.50; Seats 120; Air con; No Dogs;
Valet parking available for guests
🛏 95 Rooms; S £323-£382,
D £464-£558

A conservatory restaurant with a glass roof reminiscent of the Brighton Pavilion is the atmospheric venue for a classic English afternoon event. The Chinoiserie theme, emphasised by large potted palms and delicate flower arrangements, creates a bright and welcoming setting at teatime. While a pianist plays in the background, guests can help themselves to a pot of tea whose water has been heated by a traditional Russian Samovar packed with burning pine-cones. A simple selection of sandwiches or scones and pastries can be picked for a D tea, or 'the full Monty' comes in the form the Lanesborough, or the Belgravia – delightful extravagance at £32.

RECOMMENDED IN THE AREA
Hyde Park; Harrods; Bond Street

*T*he Lowndes Hotel ★★★★

Reassuringly traditional afternoon teas in a stylish setting

☏ 020 7823 1234
🖷 020 7235 1154
✉ contact@lowndeshotel.com
🌐 www.lowndeshotel.com

Map ref 3 - TQ37

21 Lowndes Street, LONDON,
SW1X 9ES
*M4 onto A4 into London. Left from
Brompton Rd into Sloane St. Left into
Pont St and Lowndes St next left.
Hotel on right.*
🍵 Tea served 3pm-6pm daily; Closed
25 Dec; Set tea price(s) £14.50;
🛏 78 Rooms, D £185

A boutique hotel with a very upmarket address – The Lowndes is within walking distance of Harrods and Harvey Nichols. After a hectic shopping spree, or a tour of the capital, the classic afternoon tea served in the Citronelle or lobby lounge will come as a refreshing pick-me-up. For a fixed price you can indulge in finger sandwiches, fresh scones with Cornish clotted cream and preserves, a variety of cakes, and a pot of one of a dozen teas. Coffee drinkers a also generously accommodated, and there is a choice tantalising desserts if the whole set tea package is to intimidating.

RECOMMENDED IN THE AREA
Tate Britain; Science Museum; Royal Mews

WALK

Explore London's bustling riverside and visit the famous Globe Theatre on this varied walk along the South Bank

From Somerset House head for Lancaster Place and walk towards Waterloo Bridge. Don't cross the bridge. Instead, follow the Thames upstream, keeping Britain's most famous river on your left. Pass Cleopatra's Needle, the famous 186-ton obelisk brought here from Alexandria in 1878, and continue along the Embankment in the direction of Hungerford Bridge. Cross it via the right-hand footbridge which offers a view of Westminster Bridge and Big Ben not seen for more than 100 years. Even closer is the familiar outline of the London Eye.

Join the Thames Path and head downstream towards Waterloo Bridge. Pass the Royal Festival Hall and the National Theatre and keep ahead along the riverbank to reach Gabriel's Wharf. Spend a few minutes looking at its colourful market stalls. Make for the Oxo Tower and look for the remains of an old wharf to the right of it. Pass under Blackfriars Bridge; between the road bridge and the railway bridge you'll spot the crest of the London, Chatham and Dover

railway, dated 1864. Walk along to Tate Modern and just beyond it is the Globe Theatre. Once a famous power station, Tate Modern was transformed into the world's largest modern art gallery by Herzog and de Meuron in 2000. The Globe might be a replica but it serves as a lasting memorial to the genius of one man - William Shakespeare. The original theatre was destroyed by fire in 1613. It was the actor Sam Wanamaker who campaigned to have the Globe rebuilt. His efforts eventually paid off and the new Globe was completed in 1994. Cross the Thames via the Millennium Bridge, designed by Norman Foster to link Tate Modern and St Paul's Cathedral, turn left on reaching the City bank and follow the path to Blackfriars tube and mainline stations.

DISTANCE: 2 miles/3.2km
START: Somerset House
FINISH : Blackfriars
MAP: AA Street by Street London
TERRAIN : Pavements, Embankment and riverside promenade
GRADIENT: Level ground

*M*andarin Oriental Hyde Park ★★★★★ ◎◎◎◎
An elegant hotel in the heart of Knightsbridge

📞 020 7235 2000　📠 020 7235 2001
✉ molon-reservations@mohg.com
🌐 www.mandarinoriental.com

Map ref 3 - TQ37

66 Knightsbridge, LONDON, SW1X 7LA
Harrods on right, hotel 0.5m on left opp Harvey Nichols.
🍽 Open daily; Tea served 3pm-6pm (3.30pm-6pm at weekends); Booking advisable at weekends; Set tea price(s) £23.00, £26.00; Seats 100; Air con; 🛏 200 Rooms; S £255, D £305

*O*ne of London's grandest hotels, built in 1898 Mandarin Oriental Hyde Park boasts views of both Hyde Park and Knightsbridge. Afternoon tea is served in The Park Restaurant, where every table enjoys a park view. This restaurant is also open for breakfast, lunch and dinner, with dishes from around the world. Traditional afternoon tea offers assorted finger sandwiches, freshly baked scones and tea breads with preserves, plus a choice of home-made cakes and pastries. A speciality of the house is the delicious rose petal jam. You can also order a glass of Moët & Chandon or Dom Perignon as part of a set tea. Booking advisable at weekends. No dogs.

RECOMMENDED IN THE AREA
Harrods; The Victoria & Albert Museum; Buckingham Palace

*G*rosvenor House Hotel ★★★★★
Internationally renowned hotel commandingly positioned overlooking Hyde Park

📞 0870 400 8500
📠 020 7493 3341
✉ enquiries-grosvenor@lemeridien.com
🌐 www.lemeridien-grosvenor.com

Map ref 3 - TQ37

Park Lane, LONDON, W1A 3AA
Marble Arch, halfway down Park Ln.
🍽 Open daily; Tea served 3pm-6pm daily; Booking recommended at weekends; Air con; Parking 10; 🛏 453 Rooms; S £433.58-£465.30, D £433.58-£465.30

*E*legant Edwardian interiors are the hallmark of this high society hotel, and the exclusive Park Lane location is convenient for the West End shops and theatres. Afternoon tea is served in the Park Room Lounge, overlooking Hyde Park, accompanied by live piano or harp music. The all day menu offers light dishes, snacks and desserts, morning pastries, and a set afternoon tea of finger sandwiches, pastries, mini desserts and scones. Alternatively, try the House Treat: fresh mixed berries with vanilla ice cream, fruit scones with clotted cream and strawberry preserve, and a glass of chilled Piper Heidsieck Champagne. It's a good idea to book at weekends. Guide dogs only.

RECOMMENDED IN THE AREA
Tate Modern; Buckingham Palace; The London Eye

*L*e Meridien Piccadilly ★★★★★ ◉◉

A wonderful location and an atmosphere of elegance

☎ 0870 400 8400
✆ 020 7437 3574
𝕎 www.lemeridien.com

Map ref 3 - TQ37

21 Piccadilly, LONDON, W1J 0BH
*At the Piccadilly Circus end of Piccadilly, just along the road from the Royal Academy.
Nearest tube stations are Piccadilly Circus and Green Park*

☕ Please telephone for details of tea times and prices
🛏 266 Rooms; Please telephone for room rates

As we went to press, a major refurbishment was taking place at this five star hotel, and tea was not being served. However, it was planned that tea will be available later in the year, so please telephone for up to date information.

In the past, tea has been offered in the Oak Room Lounge, an elegant Edwardian room with pale oak panelling and Venetian chandeliers, but it is likely that in future the venue will be upstairs in the stylish Terrace Restaurant. You can be sure that wherever tea is served will be a haven from the noise and bustle of London's shopping centre. The hotel enjoys a wonderful location in Piccadilly, close to the Royal Academy and convenient for Regent Street and London's theatres.

RECOMMENDED IN THE AREA
*The Royal Academy; Burlington Arcade;
Soho and theatres.*

---

*M*illennium Bailey's Hotel London Kensington ★★★★

modernised Victorian hotel where, happily, some things never change

☎ 020 7373 6000
✆ 020 7370 3760
✉ baileys@mill-cop.com
𝕎 www.millenniumhotels.com

Map ref 3 - TQ37

140 Gloucester Road, LONDON, SW7 4QH
M4, turn right at Cromwell Hospital into Knaresborough Place, follow to Courtfield Rd to corner of Gloucester Rd, hotel opposite tube station.

☕ Open daily; Tea served 3pm-5pm daily; Set tea price(s) £10.50, £15.00; Seats 24; Air con
🛏 212 Rooms; S £135-£411, D £411

Olive's Bar at Bailey's serves cool and contemporary cocktails, state-of-the-art sandwiches, tasty light bites and snacks from mid-morning to late. But if you turn up between 3 and 4.30pm, the chances are that you'll be heading for the afternoon tea menu. In the cosmopolitan atmosphere of Olive's, this institution is taken with reassuring seriousness. Expect a traditional tea and bearing finger sandwiches, patisseries, scones with clotted cream and jam, and a refreshing choice of teas. Variations on the theme include the Champagne afternoon tea or, for the fainthearted, a modest though delicious selection of pastries.

RECOMMENDED IN THE AREA
*Natural History Museum; Science Museum;
Victoria & Albert Museum*

99

*T*he Milestone ★★★★★

A popular small hotel in the heart of Royal London where tea is a time-honoured treat

☎ 020 7917 1000
📠 020 7917 1010
✉ guestservicems@rchmail.com
🌐 www.milestonehotel.com

Map ref 3 - TQ37

1 Kensington Court, LONDON, W8 5DL
Opposite Kensington Palace & Gardens.
☕ Tea served 3pm-6pm daily; Booking required; Set tea price(s) £12.50-£21.50; Seats 20; Air con
🛏 57 Rooms; S £306-£952, D £306-£952

*E*xpect to be treated like royalty at this luxurious hotel overlooking Kensington Palace and Gardens – their motto is 'no request too large, no detail too small'. The Park Lounge enjoys magnificent views of the royal property, and with its roaring fire on cooler days and stately home atmosphere at all times, it is the perfect place in which to enjoy afternoon tea. Come with friends for a chat, or curl up on your own with a good book or newspaper, and relax as you enjoy the expert service. Tea comes in a variety of flavours from Darjeeling to chamomile, accompanied by an assortment of traditional foods; with the Cream Tea come freshly-baked scones with Devonshire clotted cream and strawberry preserve, while the Afternoon Tea includes a selection of finger sandwiches (smoked salmon on honey and sultana bread perhaps), scones and French pastries. For the added touch of luxury you can enjoy a glass of champagne while your tea brews. Other light meals and drinks are also served, and booking is essential.

RECOMMENDED IN THE AREA

Commonwealth Institute; Linley Sambourne House; Science Museum

The Montague on the Gardens ★★★★ ◉

Georgian-fronted hotel serving classy teas

☎ 020 7637 1001
📠 020 7637 2516
📧 bookmt@rchmail.com
🌐 www.redcarnationshotels.com

Map ref 3 - TQ37

15 Montague Street, Bloomsbury,
LONDON, WC1B 5BJ
Next to British Museum.
☕ Open daily; Tea served 3pm-6pm;
Booking recommended; Set tea
price(s) £8.50. £9.50, £10.50, £17.00;
Seats 10; No Smoking; Air con
🛏 104 Rooms; S £158-£212,
D £176-£246

*A*n intimate atmosphere pervades this townhouse which feels more like a country hotel than one in central London. The beautiful gardens help to foster this impression, while indoors the stylish public rooms are staffed by a dedicated and discreet team. Tea in the conservatory is not to be missed, with views onto the grounds beyond; or you can go one better in the summer, and sit on the terrace under a large sunshade. A classic afternoon selection of finger sandwiches, scones and pastries served on a silver cake stand with elegant china plates and tea cups is a reminder of past grandeurs.

RECOMMENDED IN THE AREA

British Museum; London's Transport Museum; The Charles Dickens Museum

---

The Ritz ★★★★★ ◉◉

Quintessentially the Ritz experience, but advance planning is vital

☎ 020 7493 8181
📠 020 7493 2687
📧 enquire@theritzlondon.com
🌐 www.theritzlondon.com

Map ref 3 - TQ37

150 Piccadilly, LONDON, W1J 9BR
From Hyde Park Corner E on Piccadilly. Hotel on right after Green Park.
☕ Open daily; Tea served 12.00pm, 1.30pm, 3.30pm, 5.30pm; Booking required - at least 6 weeks in advance; Set tea price(s) £32; Seats 47; No smoking; Air con;
🛏 133 Rooms; S £300, D £360

*I*t's what afternoons were made for, according to London's glitzy Ritz Hotel, and their invitation to tea is one that few will forget in a hurry. Smart clothes are necessary (jeans just won't do, and men should wear a jacket and tie), and so is booking up to three months in advance, slightly less during the week. The spectacular Palm Court makes an elegant setting for the well-dressed diners, and serves a tea to match: finely cut sandwiches without a crust in sight, freshly-baked scones with jam and clotted cream, delicate pastries and a choice of seven varieties of tea, at a Ritzy price of around £60 for two. Champagne is extra.

Winner of The Tea Guild's Top London Afternoon Tea Award 2004.

RECOMMENDED IN THE AREA

Buckingham Palace; Royal Academy of Arts; Piccadilly Circus

101

*T*he Royal Horseguards Hotel ★★★★

Majestic hotel in the heart of Whitehall

☎ 020 7839 3400
🖷 020 7925 2263
✉ royalhorseguards@thistle.com
🌐 www.thistlehotels.com

Map ref 3 - TQ37

Whitehall Court, LONDON, SW1A 2EJ
🍽 Open daily; Tea served 3pm-6pm;
Booking possible; Set tea price(s)
£9.50-£14.50; Seats 30; Air con;
🛏 280 Rooms

*S*ituated right at the seat of power, close to the Prime Minister's residence, government offices, Parliament, the House of Lords and Westminster Abbey, this impressive hotel on 10 floors also offers fine views of the River Thames and the capital's skyline. Westminster Tea (fruit scones with clotted cream and preserves, and fruitcake) and Royal Horseguards Tea (as the Westminster, with the addition of delicate finger sandwiches) is served in the lounge, where a pianist plays from 6pm. The menu also offers snacks and salads, speciality sandwiches, 'Elevenses', hot dishes and sweets. Guests can also sit out in the terrace garden, weather permitting. Children welcome. Guide dogs only.

RECOMMENDED IN THE AREA

Buckingham Palace; The London Eye; Houses of Parliament

---

*R*ubens at the Palace ★★★★ ◉◉

A friendly hotel where afternoons are spent rewardingly

☎ 020 7834 6600
🖷 020 7233 6037
✉ bookrb@rchmail.com
🌐 www.redcarnationhotels.com

Map ref 3 - TQ37

39 Buckingham Palace Road,
LONDON, SW1W 0PS
Opposite Royal Mews, 100mtrs from Buckingham Palace.
🍽 Tea served 2.30pm-5pm daily;
Booking possible; Set tea price(s)
£14.50; Seats 28; Air con; Guide dogs only
🛏 173 Rooms; S £200-£530,
D £235-£530

*L*ocated directly opposite the mews of Buckingham Palace as its name suggests, this well-regarded hotel offers stylish comfort in a busy tourist area. Enter its portals greeted by a smart commissionaire, and head for the Palace Lounge and Bar where light meals are served during the day. Everything doesn't quite stop for tea, but you feel it would if it had to! The Full Afternoon set meal incorporates finger sandwiches, scones, pastries, fruit cake, and a pot of tea chosen from a range that includes Orange Pekoe, Lapsang Suchong, and that ubiquitous favourite, Earl Grey. The warm, relaxing colours and background music ensure you will be in no hurry to leave.

RECOMMENDED IN THE AREA

Buckingham Palace; Hyde Park; Oxford Street

*T*he Royal Garden Hotel ★★★★★ ◉◉◉

*Landmark modern hotel next to Hyde Park and
the Royal Gardens of Kensington Palace*

☎ 020 7937 8000   🖷 020 7361 1991
✉ sales@royalgardenhotel.co.uk   🌐 www.royalgardenhotel.co.uk

Map ref 3 - TQ37

2-24 Kensington High Street, LONDON, W8 4PT
next to Kensington Palace.
☕ Open daily; Tea served 2.30pm-5.30pm; Booking possible; Set tea price(s) £16.75;
Seats 32; Air con; 🛏 396 Rooms; S £288, D £358

RECOMMENDED IN THE AREA
*Kensington Palace; Victoria & Albert Museum;
Science Museum*

*R*enowned for its breathtaking views of the London skyline, particularly from its restaurant on the 10th floor, The Royal Garden takes its name from the neighbouring Kensington Palace Gardens. It is a comfortably modern hotel, easy on the eye, with an elegant foyer creating the perfect first impression for an afternoon tea with some cachet. The location is convenient both for Hyde Park and the smart Kensington shops, and is within walking distance of the Royal Albert Hall. The Park Terrace Restaurant, Café and Bar has a wonderfully open feel, with large windows looking out onto the drive and gardens of Kensington Palace. An all-day menu offers a good variety of snacks, grills, omelettes and speciality Oriental dishes. The set-price afternoon tea comprises a selection of freshly made finger sandwiches, home-made scones with clotted cream and a choice of home-made preserves, and a range of home-made cakes and pastries. Champagne is an optional extra. Parking available beneath the hotel. No dogs.

WALK

Dominating the starting point for this varied London walk are the restored Wellington Arch and the newly opened Australian war memorial. Take the subway signed Green Park and Constitution Hill and follow the path with the cycleway, horse track and road on your right. Green Park, created in 1660, lies to your left. Use the pedestrian crossing further down, level with Buckingham Palace, and walk alongside the railings. Pass the refurbished, greatly expanded Queen's Gallery and walk along Buckingham Palace Road, turning into Palace Street opposite the Royal Mews. Pass the Phoenix pub and cross Catherine Place. Continue to Wilfred St and on the corner is the Cask and Glass pub. Turn into Castle Lane, pleasantly leafy, and at Buckingham Gate cross over into Petty France. On the left are the Wellington Barracks, headquarters of the 1st Battalion of the Scots Guards. Turn right by Home Office into Palmer Street, passing St James's Park tube station, and swing left at the next junction. Follow Caxton Street to the 1960s New Scotland Yard building. Turn left here and make for the junction of Broadway and Tothill Street. Cross over to Carteret Street, glimpsing Westminster Abbey to your right, and make for Queen Anne's Gate. Turn left, walk along to Birdcage Walk, cross over and enter St James's Park. Pass over the lake and the Diana, Princess of Wales Memorial Walk to reach the Mall. Cross over into Marlborough Road and pass St James's Palace. Turn left at Cleveland Row, cross Stable Yard Road and a glance to the left at this point reveals Clarence House, for almost 50 years the much-loved home of the Queen Mother and now the London residence of the Prince of Wales. Clarence House is open to the public during the summer. Continue ahead to Green Park, turn right and follow Queen's Walk along to the tube station.

DISTANCE: 2 1/2 miles/ 4km
START : Hyde Park Corner tube station
FINISH: Green Park tube station
MAP: A good street map of London
TERRAIN : Pavements and park paths
GRADIENT: Level

Sofitel St James ★★★★

thoroughbred tea taken to the resonant strains of a harp

☎ 020 7747 2222
🖷 020 7747 2210
✉ H3144@accor-hotels.com
🌐 www.sofitel.com

Map ref 3 - TQ37

6 Waterloo Place, LONDON, SW1Y 4AN
On corner of Pall Mall & Waterloo Place.

Tea served 2.30pm-5.30pm daily;
Booking possible; Set tea price(s) £23.50,
£28.50; Seats 18; Air con;
186 Rooms; £320 (room only) + VAT

Afternoon tea, so the menu of the Rose Lounge informs its visitors, first became fashionable in the 1840s, 200 years after the first tea was brought to Britain from China. That it is now firmly established as a national tradition is incontestable, though few establishments include a glass of rosé champagne in their set tea as does the Sofitel Hotel (non-alcoholic version is also available!). A harpist playing in the small lounge harks back to a more gracious era, and against this classy musical background the tea ritual itself is equally reassuring and refined. Healthy appetites are necessary for a tea that includes a selection of finger sandwiches, followed by freshly-baked warm scone and crumpets with Devonshire clotted cream and jam, then a range of English and French pastries, a choice of home-made cakes, and a pot of tea or freshly-ground coffee. A lengthy list of cocktails, martinis, champagnes, wines and other drinks, along with tasty bar snacks, means that tea can happily develop into an entire evening.

RECOMMENDED IN THE AREA
National Gallery; Cabinet War Rooms; London Eye

*T*he Washington Mayfair Hotel ★★★★

Tea accompanied by wonderful hospitality and service

☎ 020 7499 7000
✆ 020 7495 6172
✉ food@
washington-mayfair.co.uk
ⓦ www.washington-
mayfair.co.uk

Map ref 3 - TQ37

5 Curzon Street, Mayfair, LONDON,
W1J 5HE
Green Park station take Piccadilly exi
and turn right. Take 4th street on righ
into Curzon St.
🍵 Open daily; Tea served 3pm-5pm
Booking possible; Set tea price(s)
£5.50, £9.50, £14.95; Seats 35; Air
con; No dogs
🛏; 171 Rooms; S £188-£235,
D £188-£235

Chic Mayfair is the salubrious setting for this upmarket modern hotel. Located just a stone's throw from the West End shopping streets, it remains faithful to its elegant early 20th-century origins. Its art deco designs can be admired in the marbled and wood-panelled public rooms, where the staff are always on hand to offer service with a smile. For afternoon tea you should head to the Madison Bar where a delicious choice awaits you: the full Mayfair Tea, with or without a glass of champagne, includes sandwiches, scones with Cornish clotted cream an preserves, and a selection of fresh pastri and cakes, with a refreshing pot of special tea.

RECOMMENDED IN THE AREA

Royal Academy of Arts;
Buckingham Palace; Bond Street

London Hotels

These hotels also offer afternoon tea. Remember you may have to book, so please telephone in advance to avoid disappointment.

★ ★ ★ ★ **Radisson Edwardian Marlborough Hotel**
Bloomsbury Street WC1B 3QD
☎ 020 7636 5601 ▤ 020 7636 0532
e: resmarl@radisson.com

★ ★ ★ ★ **De Vere Cavendish St James's, London**
81 Jermyn Street SW1Y 6JF
☎ 020 7930 2111 ▤ 020 7839 2125
e: cavendish.reservations@
devere-hotels.com

★ ★ ★ ★ **The Stafford**
16-18 St James's Place SW1A 1NJ
☎ 020 7493 0111 ▤ 020 7493 7121
e: info@thestaffordhotel.co.uk

★ ★ ★ ★ **Millennium Gloucester Hotel London Kensington**
4-18 Harrington Gardens SW7 4LH
☎ 020 7373 6030 ▤ 020 7373 0409
e: sales.gloucester@mill-cop.com

★ ★ ★ ★ **The Rembrandt**
11 Thurloe Place SW7 2RS
☎ 020 7589 8100 ▤ 020 7225 3363
e: rembrandt@sarova.co.uk

★ ★ ★ ★ **Brown's Hotel**
Albemarle Street Mayfair
W1S 4BP
☎ 020 7493 6020 ▤ 020 7493 9381
e: brownshotel@brownshotel.com

★ ★ ★ ★ **London Marriott Hotel, Grosvenor Square**
Grosvenor Square W1K 6JP
☎ 020 7493 1232 ▤ 020 7491 3201
e: businesscentre@
londonmariott.co.uk

★ ★ ★ ★ **Montcalm-Hotel Nikko London**
Great Cumberland Place
W1H 7TW
☎ 020 7402 4288 ▤ 020 7724 9180
e: reservations@montcalm.co.uk

★ ★ ★ ★ **Radisson SAS Portman Hotel**
22 Portman Square W1H 7BG
☎ 020 7208 6000 ▤ 020 7208 6001
e: sales.london@radissonsas.com

★ ★ ★ ★ **The Westbury Hotel**
Bond Street W1S 2YF
☎ 020 7629 7755 ▤ 020 7495 1163
e: reservations@
westburymayfair.com

★ ★ ★ ★ **The Chesterfield Mayfair**
35 Charles Street Mayfair
W1J 5EB
☎ 020 7491 2622 ▤ 020 7491 4793
e: bookch@rchmail.com

★ ★ ★ ★ **Jurys Clifton-Ford Hotel**
47 Welbeck Street W1M 8DN
☎ 020 7486 6600 ▤ 020 7486 7492
e: cliftonford@jurysdoyle.com

★ ★ ★ ★ **Royal Lancaster Hotel**
Lancaster Terrace W2 2TY
☎ 020 7262 6737 ▤ 020 7724 3191
e: book@royallancaster.com

★ ★ ★ ★ **Copthorne Tara Hotel London Kensington**
Scarsdale Place
Wrights Lane W8 5SR
☎ 020 7937 7211 ▤ 020 7937 7100
e: tara.sales@mill-cop.com

★ ★ ★ ★ **Le Meridien Russell**
Russell Square WC1B 5BE
☎ 020 7837 6470 ▤ 020 7837 2857

★ ★ ★ ★ **Cannizaro House**
West Side
Wimbledon Common SW19 4UE
☎ 0870 333 9124 ▤ 0870 333 9224
e: cannizarohouse@thistle.co.uk

★ ★ ★ ★ **Radisson Edwardian Grafton Hotel**
130 Tottenham Court Road
W1T 5AY
☎ 020 7388 4131 ▤ 020 7387 7394
e: resgraf@radisson.com

★ ★ ★ ★ **Radisson Edwardian Mountbatten Hotel**
Monmouth Street
Seven Dials WC2H 9HD
☎ 020 7836 4300 ▤ 020 7240 3540
e: resmoun@radisson.com

★ ★ ★ ★ **Radisson Edwardian Vanderbilt Hotel**
68-86 Cromwell Road SW7 5BT
☎ 020 7761 9000 ▤ 020 7761 9001
e: resvand@radisson.com

★ ★ ★ ★ **Radisson Edwardian Berkshire Hotel**
350 Oxford Street W1N 0BY
☎ 020 7629 7474 ▤ 020 7629 8156
e: resberk@radisson.com

★ ★ ★ ★ **Millennium Hotel London Knightsbridge**
17 Sloane Street
Knightsbridge SW1X 9NU
☎ 020 7235 4377 ▤ 020 7235 3705
e: knightsbridge.reservations@
mill.cop.com

★ ★ ★ ★ **The Abbey Court Townhouse Hotel**
20 Pembridge Gardens
Kensington W2 4DU
☎ 020 7221 7518 ▤ 020 7792 0858
e: info@abbeycourthotel.co.uk

★ ★ ★ ★ **Harrington Hall**
5-25 Harrington Gardens SW7 4JN
☎ 020 7396 9696 ▤ 020 7396 9090
e: sales@harringtonhall.co.uk

★★★★ Jurys Kensington Hotel
109-113 Queensgate South
Kensington SW7 5LR
☎ 020 7589 6300 ▤ 020 7581 1492
e: Kensington@jurysdoyle.com

★★★★ The Cranley Hotel
10 Bina Gardens South Kensington
SW5 0LA
☎ 020 7373 0123 ▤ 020 7373 9497
e: info@thecranley.com

★★★★ Grange Blooms Hotel
7 Montague Street WC1B 5BP
☎ 020 7323 1717 ▤ 020 7636 6498
e: blooms@grangehotels.com

★★★★ Kingsway Hall
Great Queen Street Covent Garden
WC2B 5BZ
☎ 020 7309 0909 ▤ 020 7309 9696
e: enquiries@kingswayhall.co.uk

★★★★ The Cadogan Hotel
75 Sloane Street SW1X 9SG
☎ 020 7235 7141 ▤ 020 7245 0994
e: info@cadogan.com

★★★★ Sheraton Belgravia
20 Chesham Place SW1X 8HQ
☎ 020 7235 6040 ▤ 020 7259 6243
e: judy-kent@sheraton.com

★★★★ Jurys Great Russell Street
16-22 Great Russell Street
WC1B 3NN
☎ 020 7347 1000 ▤ 020 7347 1001
e: sales@jurysdoyle.com

★★★★ Grange Fitzrovia
20-28 Bolsover Street W1W 5NB
☎ 020 7467 7000 ▤ 020 7636 5085
e: fitzrovia@grangehotels.com

★★★★ Kensington House Hotel
15-16 Prince of Wales Terrace
W8 5PQ
☎ 020 7937 2345 ▤ 020 7368 6700
e: sales@kenhouse.com

★★★★★ The Capital
Basil Street Knightsbridge SW3 1AT
☎ 020 7589 5171 ▤ 020 7225 0011
e: reservations@capitalhotel.co.uk

★★★★★ Claridge's
Brook Street W1A 2JQ
☎ 020 7629 8860 ▤ 020 7499 2210
e: info@claridges.co.uk

★★★★★ The Connaught
Carlos Place W1K 2AL
☎ 020 7499 7070 ▤ 020 7495 3262
e: info@the-connaught.co.uk

★★★★★ Radisson Edwardian May Fair Hotel
Stratton Street W1J 8LL
☎ 020 7629 7777 ▤ 020 7629 1459
e: mayfair@interconti.com

★★★★★ The Savoy
Strand WC2R 0EU
☎ 020 7836 4343 ▤ 020 7240 6040
e: info@the-savoy.co.uk

★★★★★ Le Meridien Waldorf
Aldwych WC2B 4DD
☎ 0870 400 8484 ▤ 020 7836 7244
e: reception.waldorf@
lemeridien.com

★★★★★ Conrad London Chelsea Harbour
SW10 0XG
☎ 020 7823 3000 ▤ 020 7351 6525
e: conrad-london@hilton.com

★★★★★ Radisson Edwardian Hampshire Hotel
31 Leicester Square WC2H 7LH
☎ 020 7839 9399 ▤ 020 7930 8122
e: reshamp@radisson.com

★★★★★ The Landmark London
222 Marylebone Road NW1 6JQ
☎ 020 7631 8000 ▤ 020 7631 8080
e:reservations@thelandmark.co.uk

★★★★★ Sheraton Park Tower
101 Knightsbridge SW1X 7RN
☎ 020 7235 8050 ▤ 020 7235 8231
e:anne.scott@luxurycollection.com

★★★★★ London Marriott Hotel, County Hall
Westminster Bridge Road County
Hall SE1 7PB
☎ 020 7928 5200 ▤ 020 7928 5300

★★★★★ Great Eastern Hotel
Liverpool Street EC2M 7QN
☎ 020 7618 5000 ▤ 020 7618 5001
e: sales@great-eastern hotel.co.uk
e: info@claridges.co.uk

★★★★★ Four Seasons Hotel Canary Wharf
Westferry Circus Canary Wharf
E14 8RS
☎ 020 7510 1999 ▤ 020 7510 1998

★★★★★ Renaissance Chancery Court London
252 High Holborn WC1V 7EN
☎ 020 7829 9888 ▤ 020 7829 9889
e: sales.chancerycourt@
renaissancehotels.com

★★★★ The Chamberlain Hotel
130-135 Minories EC3N 1NU
☎ 020 7680 1500 ▤ 020 7702 2500
e: thechamberlain@fullers.co.uk

★★★★★ Swissotel London, The Howard
Temple Place WC2R 2PR
☎ 020 7836 3555 ▤ 020 7379 4547
e: us.london@swissotel.com

Norfolk

The two foods most closely associated with Norfolk are probably turkeys and mustard, the latter grown in fields around the county town of Norwich, and both a useful addition to a sandwich. A not-to-be-missed treat when visiting the Norfolk coast, however, is the estimable Cromer crab. Norfolk has its own take on the treacle tart, which doesn't include any breadcrumbs, but rather mixes golden syrup with eggs and cream for its characteristically creamy filling. Norfolk rusks are another regional speciality, similar to Suffolk rusks, though connoisseurs may say that the Norfolk version is a little less rich.

Norfolk and Suffolk also have a regional approach to dumplings, which they make with a bread dough rather than a suet mix. The resulting dumplings are rather lighter, floating on the stew rather than sinking into it.

Margaret's Tea Rooms

Farmhouse tea rooms in a charming village setting

☎ 01263 577614

Map ref 4 - TG13

Chestnut Farmhouse, The Street, BACONSTHORPE, Holt, NR25 6AB
🍵 Open 10.30am-5pm Mothering Sunday-end Oct. Weekends only in Nov; Tea served all day; Closed Mon, Tue; No credit cards; Seats 42 + 24 outside; No smoking; Children welcome

*A*t Chestnut Farmhouse in the village of Baconsthorpe, Margaret and Roger Bacon serve morning coffee, light lunches and afternoon tea in the Harebell, Strawberry or Rose Parlours. The tea rooms seat 42 inside with room for another 24 in the garden. Margaret makes all the breads, pastries, scones and preserves herself in the farmhouse kitchen and the selection varies from day to day. A range of 25 teas and herbal infusions is offered, along with 10 ground coffees, pure fruit juices and cordials. Home-made soups and quiches feature, and all the dishes, sandwiches, cakes and biscuits are individually priced. Parking is provided. No dogs in the house or garden.

Winner of The Tea Guild's Top Tea Place Award 2003.

The Tea Guild Award of Excellence 2004.

RECOMMENDED IN THE AREA
North Norfolk Railway; Blickling Hall; Thursford Collection

WALK

Norfolk - Blickling Hall and Itteringham

A very pleasant ramble starting at Blickling Hall, a magnificent Jacobean house surrounded by splendid parkland

After visiting Blickling Hall make for the main park gates and take the track left across the park. At a fork continue ahead and shortly the walk runs beside the Great Wood. Avoid the estate walk waymarks, pass beside a gate and keep ahead through trees to a lane by a cottage. Turn left and follow a country road across Itteringham Common to reach the Walpole Arms.

From the pub turn left, then right at the T junction, crossing the River Bure into the village of Itteringham. Take the lane signed 'village stores' and then turn immediately right, following a track beside Manor Farm. Keep ahead to a gate, veer slightly right to a stile and follow the field boundary up the slope. Turn right into the adjoining field and keep left along the field

perimeter. Follow the track beside White House Farm and shortly the walk turns left to run along the metalled access lane. Pass a cottage on the left, then on reaching a sharp right bend take the waymarked path ahead along a track. Swing left at a footpath waymark into the field and keep right, maintaining the same direction. Cross the second stile, bear left across a meadow and pass alongside woodland to reach a footbridge across the Bure. Swing slightly left across fields to another footbridge and follow the path to a metalled lane. Turn right, then left in front of Moorgate Cottages, and follow the path left around the field edge. Keep ahead to a junction by a tree seat. This is the Weavers Way. Follow the track ahead across Blickling Park, with the lake seen on the left. The house looms into view ahead along this stretch. Make for the main gates and return to the car park.

DISTANCE: 6 miles/9.7km
START/FINISH: Blickling Hall
MAP: OS Explorer 252
TERRAIN : Parkland and farmland
GRADIENT: Level

Congham Hall Country House Hotel ★★★ ◎◎

Georgian manor house a few miles from Sandringham

☎ 01485 600250
📠 01485 601191
✉ info@conghamhallhotel.co.uk
🌐 www.conghamhallhotel.co.uk

Map ref 4 - TF72

Lynn Road, GRIMSTON, King's Lynn, PE32 1AH
6m NE of King's Lynn on A148, R towards Grimston, hotel 2.5m on L (do not go to Congham).
🍵 Open daily; Tea served 12pm-6pm Booking required (for full afternoon tea); Set tea price(s) £2.50-£8.50; Seats 40; No smoking areas; Parking 50;
🛏 14 Rooms; D £165-£285

Congham Hall is a fine country house set in 30 acres of parkland, orchards, gardens and the famous herb garden stocked with 700 different herbs, including 50 varieties of mint. Log fires provide a warm welcome in the public rooms, and full afternoon tea is served in the lounge and bar, or out on the terrace in warmer weather. The set tea comprises cake, biscuits, scones and home-made preserves, cream cakes and seasonal fruit tartlets. A range of home-made produce and Norfolk delicacies is offered for sale: preserves, pot pourri, lavender, books, and herb plants (May-September). Dogs allowed on terrace. Parking provided.

RECOMMENDED IN THE AREA

Sandringham House & Grounds; Holkham Hall & Gardens; Houghton Hall & Gardens

*A*lfresco Tea Rooms

A welcoming tea shop in the scenic Norfolk Broads

☎ 01692 678384
✉ alfresco.tearooms@
   btopenworld.com

Map ref 4 - TG31

Norwich Road, LUDHAM, NR29 5AQ
*on A1062, midway between Wroxham
& Potter Heigham. Tea rooms in
centre of Ludham.*
☕ Open 10.30am-5pm; Tea served
all day; Closed Mon (ex BHs);
end Oct – mid-Mar (Mother's Day
weekend; Set tea price(s) £3.60;
Seats 24; No Smoking; No Dogs

*T*hink of a row of white, picture-postcard cottages topped with a carved thatched roof, and you have the Alfresco tea shop. The pretty village of Ludham is tucked away in the heart of the Norfolk Broads, and this delightful tea shop is a magnet for the many tourists visiting the area. Run by Daphne and John Larkins, it can be found opposite the village church. The light lunches, open sandwiches and mouth-watering cakes are all made on the premises, and

the set cream tea comes with a choice of loose leaf tea made properly in a teapot.

RECOMMENDED IN THE AREA
*Norwich Cathedral; Merrivale Model
Village; Pettitts Animal Adventure Park*

---

*T*he Tea & Coffee Shop

Fine teas, coffees and food in a modern setting

☎ 01603 760790
🖷 01603 722122

Map ref 4 - TG21

33 Orford Place, NORWICH, NR1 3QA
☕ Open daily; Tea served 9.30am-
4.30pm; Closed Sun & BHs; Seats 36;
No Smoking; Air con

*A*nyone interested in really fine teas and coffees will love this place set above a shop devoted to both beverages. Over three dozen different varieties of black, green and herbal teas can be sampled in the modern air-conditioned tea rooms, with unusual and special flavours being carefully brewed with filtered water. Coffee ground freshly from 18 beans and 11 blends offers another experience not to be missed. Light lunches in the form of Welsh rarebit, naturally-cured ham and omelettes also

appear on the menu, along with sandwiches, cakes, gateaux, fruit pies and biscuits. A shop downstairs sells teas, coffees and accessories.

RECOMMENDED IN THE AREA
*Norwich Cathedral; Bridewell Museum;
Sainsbury Centre for the Visual Arts*

Nottinghamshire

Lacemakers in Nottinghamshire, as in other parts of the country, have always celebrated St Catherine's Day, November 25, with Cattern cakes made from yeasted dough mixed with lard, sugar and caraway seeds. (St Catherine being the patron saint of lacemakers, spinners, rope makers and spinsters.)

An old favourite from the county town is Nottingham pudding. To make the dish, whole apples are cored and filled with sugar then covered with a batter pudding mixture and baked. This is a sweet version of toad in the hole, really, with apples instead of sausages.

Wheat cakes boiled in richly spiced milk is a special dish traditionally served on Christmas Eve in Nottinghamshire.

*O*ld School Tearoom

Old school artifacts and wonderful home baking

☎ 01909 483517

Map ref 8 - SK57

Carburton, WORKSOP, S80 3BP
On B6034 between Worksop & Ollerton opposite entrance to Clumber Park
☕ Open 10am-4pm (Nov-Mar), 10am-4.30pm (Apr-Oct);Tea served all day;
Closed Mon, Two weeks over Xmas & New Year; Booking possible; Set tea price(s)
fr £5.50; No credit cards; Seats 38 + 16 outside; No Smoking; Guide dogs only;
Parking 20 + off-road parking

RECOMMENDED IN THE AREA

*Clumber Park; Roche Abbey;
Wetlands Waterfowl Reserve &
Exotic Bird Park*

*T*his peaceful country tea room is housed in a converted 1930s school, where many original features have been used to delightful effect. The menu is written on an old blackboard and easel, and the original hand basins have been kept in the washrooms. Where once reference books and stacks of homework sat on the school shelves, displays of local woodwork, prints and greetings cards are now on sale. Home-baked fruit pies, cakes and scones feature on the interesting menu, and the savoury tea (cheese scones with cheese, celery and chutney) makes a tasty alternative to the set cream tea.

*L*ock House Tea Rooms

Indulge in a little culinary nostalgia with a range of old-fashioned choices

☎ 0115 972 2288

✉ mt@lockhousetearoom.demon.co.uk

Map ref 8 - SK53

Trent Lock, Lock Lane, LONG EATON,
NG10 2FY
*3 miles from M1 J24. 1 mile outside Long
Eaton at junction of River Trent & Erewash
Canal.*

☕ Open Wed-Fri 10am-4pm (winter)
10am-5pm (summer); Sat & Sun 10am-5pm
(winter) 10am-6pm (summer); Tea served all
day; Closed Mon & Tue, & 25 & 31 Dec;
Seats 30; No Smoking; No Dogs;
Parking 200

Idyllically set where the rivers Trent and Soar meet, in attractive Nottinghamshire countryside, these tea rooms specialise in good old-fashioned cooking. The house dates from 1794, and although it has been modernised over the years by successive lock keepers, there is still evidence of the blacksmith's forge and stabling for barge horses which were an early feature. A cell found beneath the house suggests that a militiaman was stationed at this busy river junction to deter would-be thieves from ransacking the laden boats. The Ashby family offer a warm welcome, and a menu to delight visitors. There's a choice of over 50 teas and a selection of speciality coffees. Choose from Cornish clotted cream teas, hot toasties, tripe and onions, jacket potatoes, and specials including rabbit pie, fresh poached salmon, and various salads, as well as the famous prawn tea. Relish the knickerbocker glory – reputedly the largest for miles around. Attached to the tea rooms is an antique and gift shop.

The Tea Guild Award of Excellence 2004.

RECOMMENDED IN THE AREA
*Nottingham Lace Centre; Royal Crown Derby
Visitor Centre; Donington Grand Prix Collection*

*O*llerton Watermill Tea Shop

The only working watermill in Nottinghamshire, with a delightful tea shop serving delicious wholesome food

☎ 01623 824094

Map ref 8 - SK67

OLLERTON, NG22 9AA
Village centre.
☕ Open 10.30am-5pm; Tea served all day; Closed Mon, Tue & Jan & Feb; Set tea price(s) £3.50; No credit cards; Seats 34; No Smoking

*T*he old millwright's workshop and watermill, built in 1713 and now fully operational, is the wonderfully atmospheric setting for this friendly tea shop. The old mill has been put to work again since the Mettam family – owners and millers since 1921 – decided to restore it and open it to the public. The teashop was an inspirational stroke of genius when it was set up to offer refreshments to mill visitors, and its popularity quickly soared. Sisters-in-law Kate and Ellen Mettam are particular about the produce that goes into their menu, and the result is home-baked cakes, quiches, salads and mouth-watering puddings; the cream tea with its three plain or fruit scones, jam, cream and strawberries is a perennial winner. The views from the window looking upstream to the waterwheel and mill race are delightful. For those who want to learn a little about the working life of the 18th-century miller, this lovely spot is the perfect place.

The Tea Guild Award of Excellence 2004.

RECOMMENDED IN THE AREA

Rufford Abbey & Park; Sherwood Forest Farm Park; Ancient Market Town of Newark

Oxfordshire

Banbury cakes, puff pastry ovals filled with a fruity mixture are similar to Eccles cakes and Chorley cakes, though some versions of the recipe call for the addition of rum. They have been made for centuries and at one time they were sold on the street from special lidded baskets. Some say the cakes date back to pagan times and are associated with May Day celebrations.

Oxford marmalade has a distinctively dark amber colouring. It is thickly cut and the flavour is a little more bitter than that of other marmalades.

Oxford sausages are packed with pork, veal, suet, lemon and herbs and are generally made without a skin.

Old Parsonage Hotel ★★★★

For guests at this smart and welcoming hotel afternoon tea is a definite priority

☎ 01865 310210
🖷 01865 311262
🄴 info@oldparsonage-hotel.co.uk
🆆 www.oxford-hotels-restaurants.co.uk/op.html

Map ref 3 - SP50

1 Banbury Road, OXFORD, OX2 6NN
From Oxford ring road to city centre via Summertown. Hotel last building on right next to St Giles Church before city centre.
🍴 Tea served 3pm-5.30pm daily; Closed 24-27 Dec; Set tea price(s) £6.00-£11.00; Seats 32 + 40 (terrace); Air con; No Dogs;
🛏 30 Rooms; S £125, D £135-£195

*T*his beautiful townhouse hotel dates in part from the 16th century, and offers comfortable seating areas for day visitors. Afternoon tea is served in the cosy club-like restaurant, or on the terrace of one of the two small garden areas on warm summer days. A special menu offers a choice of Parson's Light Tea (scones with cream and preserves, various teas including the Old Parsonage Blend, and coffees), or Traditional Afternoon Tea (sandwich, home-baked cakes, and scones with cream and preserves, and tea/coffee). Other teatime offerings include toasted crumpets, home-made ice creams and sorbets, and hot chocolate or toddy to keep out the winter chill.

RECOMMENDED IN THE AREA
Ashmolean Museum; Pitt Rivers Museum; Oxford Colleges; University Parks & Botanic Gardens

Shropshire

Like Herefordshire, Shropshire is an apple county. There are plenty of recipes for apple cakes, or you could try apple cobs (apples filled with honey and spices and completely encased in shortcrust pastry). Soul Cakes were made for All Soul's Day on November 2nd. Children went 'a-souling' - going from house to house chanting 'A soul-cake, a soul-cake, please, good missus, a soul-cake. One for Peter, one for Paul, and three for Him who saved us all.' The biscuit-like cakes are made with butter, sugar, eggs, flour, spices and currants, sometimes with strands of saffron as well. Welsh border tart (a meringue-topped lemon pie) and caraway soda bread are also traditional in Shropshire, as are cakes to celebrate particular times of year. The spicy 'lambing cake' kept workers going through the long cold nights when the first spring lambs were born, and 'shearing cake', a spicy rich cake with brown sugar, caraway seeds, lemon rind honey and ginger, was devoured after the shearing was finished.

*B*ird on the Rock Tearoom

Highly-regarded tea rooms serving speciality teas and delicious food, with plenty of produce to take home

☎ **01588 660631**

Map ref 2 - SO47

Abcott, CLUNGUNFORD, SY7 0PX
On B4367 between Craven Arms & Hopton Heath.

☕ Open Wed-Sun 10.30am-6pm (summer), 10.30am-5pm (winter); Tea served all day; Closed Mon & Tue (except BHs – closed days may then be Tue & Wed); Booking recommended; Set tea price(s) £4-£10.50; No credit cards; Seats 27 + 20 outside; No Smoking; No Dogs; Parking 9

Some very rare teas from small selected estates are among the connoisseur's choice offered at his popular tea shop. Russian Caravan, Yunnan, several Oolongs, Lady Grey, Nilgiri, and Keemun expand the usual specialist choice, along with the house Shropshire Blend (strong old-fashioned) and Bertie's Brew (a little fruity), and visitors are encouraged to sample some unfamiliar flavours which they might otherwise never try. On the food front, one of the set afternoon teas includes a themed selection with 'something savoury followed by something sweet', and a choice of tea or other drink. The 'Complete Jeeves', on the other hand, is just as grand as it sounds: don't be surprised to see a tiered cake stand presented at your table, piled high with sandwiches, scones and cakes (booking in advance is recommended for this choice). Seasonal tea-tasting events are a regular feature here, and home-made jams and chutneys, specially packed teas, and gifts and books are all on sale.

Winner of The Tea Guild's 'Top Tea Place 2004'.

RECOMMENDED IN THE AREA

Shropshire Hills Discovery Centre; Ludlow Castle; Burford House & Gardens

WALK

Shropshire - Ludlow

Enjoy this pleasant walk in the fields and pastures below the hilltop town of Ludlow

Make for the castle entrance in the centre of Ludlow, keep right of it and follow the Mortimer Trail down to Dinham Bridge over the River Teme. Cross over and follow the road round to the right. Pass a row of stone cottages and then take the lane signed Priors Halton. Swing right just before the Cliffe Hotel and go diagonally right in the field towards woodland. Descend steeply to a stile in the field corner, cross a footbridge and a second stile and keep right in the next field. Make

for the next stile and keep ahead for some time until you draw level with a farm over to the left. Turn left to a waymark, a footbridge and a stile in the boundary and then head slightly right. Cross into the next field, maintain the same direction and join a grassy track in the corner. Turn right after a few paces and follow a firm track towards Bromfield. On reaching the A49 turn right, re-cross the Teme and pass the Cookhouse pub. Follow the A49, turning right just beyond the Bromfield

village sign to follow a bridleway running parallel to the road. Keep on the grassy track to a bridleway sign by a road junction and turn right. Follow the Shropshire Way south, pass under power lines and swing left at the next waymark. Keep Ludlow church tower ahead in the distance and pass to the right of some farm outbuildings. Join a track and continue to the next farm buildings. Cross an intersection, make for a gate and waymark and pass a school. The track graduates to a tarmac lane before reaching the road. Turn right towards Ludlow town centre, then right at a bus stop and head diagonally left across the field, in line with Ludlow Castle. Go through a kissing gate into the next pasture and cross a footbridge. Make for the next gate and footbridge and walk along to the road. Go straight ahead and when the road curves right, keep ahead. Climb some steps, turn left into Upper Linney, then right to the parish church of St Laurence. From the church make for Ludlow town centre.

DISTANCE: 6 miles/9.7km
START/FINISH: Ludlow
MAP: OS Explorer 203
TERRAIN : Fields and pasture
GRADIENT: Mainly flat

*D*e Grey's

An old-fashioned bakery and tea shop serving a wide choice of pastries, cakes and speciality teas

☎ 01584 872764
✉ info@degreys.co.uk
🌐 www.degreys.co.uk

Map ref 2 - SO57

5-6 Broad Street, LUDLOW, SY8 1NG
In the centre of town, below the Buttercross clock tower in Broad Street.

☕ Open Mon-Thurs 9am-5pm, Fri & Sat 9am-5.30pm, Sun 11am-5pm; Tea served all day; Closed 26 Dec & 1 Jan; Booking possible; Set tea price(s) £7.25-£8.25; Seats 105 (winter) 135 (summer); Guide dogs only

Located just below the Buttercross clock tower in the centre of this medieval town, De Grey's is housed behind a picturesquely-beamed bakery and cake shop. Produce for sale here also includes chocolates, coffees, jams, biscuits and chutneys – all home-made – as well as a very large range of teas. Inside the tea shop you can sample a thoroughly decent brew of speciality tea, or try an iced green and mandarin tea, or perhaps wild blackberry and apple. For the hungry there is a splendid afternoon tea consisting of sandwich of choice, fancy cake, and fruit scone with jam and cream, or you can pick your own selection from toasted teacake, pastries, scones and buns. Light and full meals are served throughout the day; the menu includes Welsh rarebit or club sandwiches, as well as home-made lasagne, roasted duck confit, salads and baked potatoes. In fine weather, the patio with tables and chairs comes into its own.

The Tea Guild Award of Excellence 2004.

RECOMMENDED IN THE AREA
Ludlow Castle; Shropshire Hills Discovery Centre; Stokesay Castle

Somerset

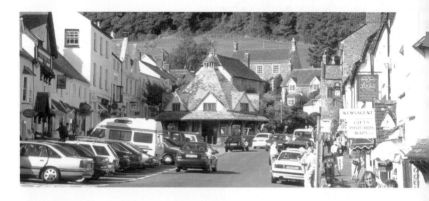

The most popular and widely consumed British cheese is unquestionably the great Cheddar from Somerset. The cheese was once made on many of the farms in the vicinity of the village of Cheddar, but today there is only one manufacturer remaining in the birthplace of the cheese, the Cheddar Gorge Cheese Company, though of course there are many other Cheddar makers in country. Visitors to the factory can see the whole process of traditional cheese making from start to finish. Cheese making in Somerset is not restricted to its native Cheddar, however, as an award winning Somerset Brie is made from local milk by Lubborn Cheese Ltd at Cricket St Thomas. Cider-making is also very much a part of the Somerset heritage. At one time every farm would grow cider apples and have its own press producing 'scrumpy' for home consumption. These days cider making is a more commercial enterprise, though some small companies are still making cider in the traditional way. Recently the county has also seen a revival of cider-brandy making.

The city of Bath is famous for two kinds of buns, Bath Buns and Sally Lunns. The former are traditionally flavoured with caraway seeds (but these days are more likely to be filled with currants), and topped with crushed sugar. Sally Lunns are rich, light and generously proportioned brioche-type buns, which can be served with sweet or savoury accompaniments. The buns can still be enjoyed at Sally Lunn's Refreshment House & Museum in Bath. The original oven, Georgian cooking range and a collection of baking utensils are displayed in the museum.

*T*he Bath Spa Hotel ★★★★ ⊚⊛

Smart city hotel serving appetising teas

☎ 0870 400 8222
🖷 01225 444006
✉ sales@bathspahotel.com
🌐 www.bathspahotel.com

Map ref 2 - ST76

Sydney Road, BATH, BA2 6JF
*M4 junct 18/A46 for Bath/A4 city
centre. Left onto A36 at 1st traffic
lights. Right at mini rdbt then left into
Sydney Place. Hotel 200yds on right.*
🍵 Open daily; Tea served 2pm-5pm
daily; Booking advisable;
Set tea price(s) £9.50, £16.00; Seats
35; Parking 156;
🛏 102 Rooms; S £190-£220,
D £190-£220

A timeless elegance distinguishes this fine Georgian mansion, set close to many of the city's attractions in seven acres of pretty landscaped gardens. Its chequered history includes periods as a boys' school, a very upmarket nurses' home, and a requisitioned war office used frequently by Winston Churchill. Now restored to its former glory, it offers five-star luxury to Bath visitors. Among its hedonistic indulgences is afternoon tea, including the comprehensive 'Full' choice and the slightly lesser cream tea; both are named after former inhabitants of the city. Sandwiches, cakes, pastries, scones and cream are helped along with a fine pot of leaf tea (or coffee), served in the exquisite drawing room.

RECOMMENDED IN THE AREA

*Thermal Bath Spa; Roman Baths;
American Museum*

*T*he Lansdown Grove ★★★ ⊚

Elegant and grand, like Bath itself

☎ 01225 483888
🖷 01225 483838
✉ lansdown@
marstonhotels.com
🌐 www.marstonhotels.com

Map ref 2 - ST76

Lansdown Road, BATH, BA1 5EH
*Follow signs to Lansdown Park & Ride
& continue towards town centre. Hotel
on left.*
🍵 Open daily; Tea served All day;
Closed 25-Dec; Booking possible;
Set tea price(s) £9.50; Seats 20;
No dogs; Parking 20;
🛏 ; 60 Rooms; S £80, D £100

*A*n 18th-century hotel built from honey-coloured stone, and set in delightful gardens just a short uphill walk from the city centre. The hotel has been carefully refurbished to provide an elegant and relaxed atmosphere for guests. In these surroundings, afternoon tea has a grandeur about it that befits this Georgian city. In the Jane Austen lounge, the cocktail bar or the main bar, friends can settle comfortably around small tables and enjoy the traditional selection: scones with preserves and clotted cream, finger sandwiches and traditional cakes come with a pot of chosen tea, a hot chocolate or coffee.

RECOMMENDED IN THE AREA

*The Building of Bath Museum; Roman Baths & Pump
Room; Museum of Costume*

The Pump Room

Classical music, elegant surroundings and fine teas

☎ 01225 444477
❺ 01225 315942
**✉ carolyn.brown@
compass-group.co.uk**
ⓦ www.romanbaths.co.uk

Map ref 2 - ST76

Stall Street, BATH, BA1 1LZ
*On right facing main entrance to
Abbey.*
🏆 Open 9.30am-4pm; Tea served
2.30pm-4pm daily; Closed 25, 26
Dec; Booking possible Mon-Fri; Set
tea price(s) £9.75, £14.75; Seats 150;
No Smoking; Guide dogs only

*F*or over two centuries the great and good have come to be restored at this striking neo-classical salon. The hot spa water they came to find is still on sale here, and many swear by its healing properties. But of more interest to Bath's modern visitors is the excellent hot and cold food served here. High on the list of favourites comes afternoon tea with its much-loved choices: smoked salmon sandwiches, scones with strawberry jam and cream (plus half a bottle of champagne for the adventurous), cakes and pastries, and even cheddar and Stilton crostinis with the high tea, and live classical music to boot.

RECOMMENDED IN THE AREA
*Bath Postal Museum; Museum of Costume;
Holbourne Museum of Art*

The Royal Crescent Hotel ★★★★★ ◉◉◉

Smart surroundings for an equally graceful afternoon tea

☎ 01225 823333
❺ 01225 339401
✉ info@royalcrescent.co.uk
ⓦ www.royalcrescent.co.uk

Map ref 2 - ST76

16 Royal Crescent, BATH, BA1 2LS
*Along A4, right at traffic lights. 2nd left onto
Bennett St. Continue into the Circus, 2nd exit
onto Brock St, No.16 on cobbled street.*
🏆 Open daily; Tea served 3.30pm-5pm;
Booking required; Set tea price(s) £10.75,
£16.50, £26.00; Air con; Parking 10
🛏 45 Rooms, D £240-£840

*T*he world-famous Royal Crescent is a striking example of Georgian architecture and a landmark at the top of the city. The magnificent sweep of buildings is the setting for this elegant hotel, where a delightful garden leads to further public rooms. The grandeur of the surroundings is matched by the glamour of afternoon tea served in the mansion drawing room, or the Dower House. The simple cream tea is easily outdone by the traditional choice – sandwiches, scones with jam and cream, cakes and pastries, Bath buns, and a choice of classy teas. For special occasions a glass of champagne makes a memorable addition.

RECOMMENDED IN THE AREA
Bath city; Museums & Galleries; Thermae Bath Spa

WALK

Somerset - Exford

Follow this very attractive walk across stunning Exmoor hills. Parts of the walk are beside the pretty River Exe, with delightful stretches of tree-shaded path adding to the enjoyment

Make for a kissing gate at the end of the car park and take the path by the Exe. Head for two more kissing gates and then turn right across the river to a collection of buildings known as North Court. Turn left by Rowan Cottage and Mountain Ash Cottage and follow the bridleway. When the drive swings right, go straight on through a gate and follow the track uphill, then down alongside Court Copse. Pass through several gates, climbing steeply to a junction. Avoid the permissive path on the left and turn right towards Road Hill. Stay on the path as it runs along the right-hand edge of several fields and when you reach a fork,

keep left and head for the next waymark. Keep left at this point, following the sign for Winsford. When the track becomes no more than a grassy path, continue ahead, avoiding a gate in the right boundary. Begin the dramatic descent into a peaceful valley, keep the Exe over to your left and look for a gate and footpath in the right boundary. Follow the permissive path alongside the river to a concrete bridge. Cross it and stay on the track as it runs to the left, passing the buildings of East Nethercote. Keep ahead to adjacent West

Nethercote. Follow the track via a series of gates, using the parallel path if wet underfoot. Keep right at a fork and climb above the river. Pass the buildings of Lyncombe and go through a gate just beyond them. Turn left after about 20 yards and follow the path through the field, sweeping round and across the middle. Make for a stile by the riverbank, then two more. Look for some gorse bushes and cross the lower slopes of the hill. Go through a gate keeping the boundary on your right. Look for a stile in the top corner, head up the field slope and cross a stile by a sign for Higher Combe. Go forward down the track towards North Court and turn right at the sign for the church.

Cross the field to a farm and follow the drive to the road. Turn left and return to Exford.

DISTANCE: 6.5 miles/10.4km
START/FINISH: Car park at Exford
MAP: OS Explorer OL9
TERRAIN: Rolling hills and valleys on Exmoor
GRADIENT: Some steep climbing

*S*ally Lunn's

Famous tea rooms renowned for the eponymous bun

☎ 01255 461634
📠 01255 811800
✉ sallylunns@aol.com
🌐 www.sallylunns.co.uk

Map ref 2 - ST76

4 North Parade Passage, BATH, BA1 1NX
☕ Open daily; Tea served 10am-6pm;
Closed 25, 26 Dec, 1 Jan; Set tea price(s)
from £5.25; Seats 90; No Smoking; Air con;
No dogs

*R*eputedly the oldest house in Bath, Sally Lunn's was named after a young Huguenot refugee called Solange Luyon who arrived in Bath from France in 1680. Her native brioches soon took hold of the local imagination, and the rest is history. The light and creamy Sally Lunn Bun can be eaten as a whole or by the half, topped with jam and cream for a delicious tea at any time of the day, or with savouries for a filling snack. Set in a narrow street this is one of Bath's most enduring tourist attractions. Lunches and morning coffees are also on the menu, with a good choice of well-brewed teas.

RECOMMENDED IN THE AREA
Roman Baths & Pump Room; No 1 Royal Crescent; Glastonbury Tor

---

*L*ewis's Tea Rooms

Unhurried pace in an inviting old-world setting

☎ 01398 323850

Map ref 2 - SS92

13 The High Street, DULVERTON,
TA22 9HB
☕ Open daily; Tea served 10am-
5pm; Closed one week in Jan;
Booking possible; Set tea price(s)
£3.75, £4.50; No credit cards; Seats
40 + 15 outside; No Smoking

*T*his instantly welcoming tea shop occupies a pair of 18th-century cottages that have been knocked into one. At either end a stone fireplace blazes in winter, and in the summer the flower-filled courtyard tempts visitors outside. Dotted around the spacious primrose-painted room are items for sale - pottery, paintings, small antiques, dried flowers and gifts - and fresh flowers brighten the tables. Rarebits are a savoury speciality here, with quiches, pâtés, and jacket potatoes, plus home-made cakes and puddings. When it comes to teatime, the speciality loose leaf teas and fat scones with strawberry jam and clotted cream prove to be winners every time.

The Tea Guild Award of Excellence 2004.

RECOMMENDED IN THE AREA
Barrington Court Garden; Cleeve Abbey, Dunster Castle

S ton Easton Park ★ ★ ★ ★ ◉ ◉

A grand hotel perfectly suited to afternoon tea

☎ **01761 241631**
🖷 **01761 241377**
✉ **enquiries@stoneaston.co.uk**
🌐 **www.stoneaston.co.uk**

Map ref 2 - ST65

STON EASTON, BA3 4DF
On A37.
☕ Open daily; Tea served daily from 3-6pm (except 25 Dec); Booking required; Set tea price(s) £5.50, £10.50;
Seats 30; Parking 120
🛏 23 Rooms; S £120-£340, D £150-£395

A superb Palladian mansion in a romantic setting on a large private estate, this beautiful house attracts discerning visitors from all over the world. The hotel boasts everything from luxury suites to fine dining, with the sort of service expected of wealthy country houses from another era. However, few things are quite so eagerly anticipated as the afternoon ritual carried out variously in the restful library, the grand and small lounges, and the Palladian Saloon with its Eagle of Jupiter ceiling motif. A selection of finger sandwiches, fruit scones with jam and clotted cream, home-made cakes, pastries and fruit tartlets is included, with a pot of tea or coffee chosen from a select range.

RECOMMENDED IN THE AREA
City of Bath; Wells Cathedral; Glastonbury Abbey

Staffordshire

Staffordshire oatcakes are strongly identified with the potteries area of north Staffordshire. They are made from a yeasty batter of oats and flour mixed with milk and water and fried like a pancake. Oatcakes are extremely versatile and though traditionally served for breakfast with a fry up of bacon and eggs, they are equally appealing for a snack meal, used like a wrap with the filling or accompaniment of your choice, or as a dessert with a sweet filling.

Historically, oats were the staple cereal grown on the county's windswept moorlands, on the fringes of the Pennines, and oatcakes the daily bread of ordinary folk. James Boswell sampled

Staffordshire oatcakes in 1776 when he accompanied his friend Dr Samuel Johnson on a visit to Litchfield. He found them very different from the hard biscuit-like oatcake of his native Scotland. Staffordshire beef is another prime local product to look out for in the county, sometimes served beneath an oaten pastry.

Greystones 17th Century Tea Room
Home-baked food served in a relaxed tea shop

☎ 01538 398522

Map ref 7 - SJ95

23 Stockwell Street, LEEK, ST13 6DH
On A523 Buxton to Macclesfied Road next to library.

🍴 Open 10am-5pm; Tea served all day, lunch served 11.30am-3pm; Closed Mon, Tue, Thu, Sun; occasionally closed for holidays, please telephone to check; No credit cards; Seats 24; No Smoking; No Dogs

Greystones is a Grade II* listed building with mullioned windows and leaded lights, the perfect setting for morning coffee, lunch and afternoon tea. Owner Janet does all the baking and her cakes have a devoted following. Try the lemon meringue pie, the Queen Mother's favourite date and walnut pudding, or Leek gingerbread from a hundred-year-old recipe. Greystones was winner of The Tea Guild's Top Tea Room Award 2000, and **The Tea Guild's Award of**

Excellence in 1999, 2001, 2002, 2003 and 2004.

RECOMMENDED IN THE AREA
Walks, stately homes, gardens & railways in the Peak Park; Leek – James Brindley Mill, Leek Canal; indoor & outdoor market; Grade I churches

Suffolk

Suffolk rusks are a bit like scones only drier, served with butter and sweet or savoury accompaniments. They are similar to Norfolk rusks, though aficionados have it that the Suffolk version is mixed a little richer and is consequently cut smaller. Suffolk, again like its neighbouring county Norfolk, has a creamy treacle tart without any breadcrumbs in it. Suffolk syllabub is another ancient sweet, a delightful concoction of lemon, sherry and cream. Greengages, a kind of green plum, were first grown in the 18th century

by Sir William Gage in his orchards near Bury St Edmunds, and this unusual fruit is still popular in the area.

*F*lying Fifteens

Seafront tea rooms by the award-winning South Beach

☎ / ✆ 01502 581188

Map ref 4 - TM59

19a The Esplanade, LOWESTOFT, NR33 0QG

🍴 Open Etr-Spring Bank Hol - weekends only. Spring Bank Hol-mid-Sep daily; Tea served 10.30am-5pm; Closed Mon (open BHs); Seats 33 + 56 outside; No Smoking

*T*hese popular tea rooms benefit from full waitress service and a lovely garden overlooking the beach. All the food is home-cooked using the best ingredients, and chips are banned from the menu. Specialities include locally smoked salmon, honey roast Norfolk ham and, on Saturdays, fresh Cromer crab. There are no set meals, just a good choice of sandwiches, soup, omelettes, salads and cakes, with favourites such as strawberry scones, very large meringues and boozy fruitcake. The name 'Flying Fifteens' comes from a sailing boat designed by Uffa Fox in the 1940s, 'fifteen' relating to its 15-foot length. Teas, gifts and greeting cards are sold. Dogs permitted in the garden; parking close by.

The Tea Guild Award of Excellence 2004.

RECOMMENDED IN THE AREA

East Anglian Transport Museum; Lowestoft Porcelain and The Kiln; New Pleasurewood Hills

Surrey

Richmond Maids of Honour, sweet tartlets filled with an almond and lemon mixture, are thought to have originated at Hampton Court in the 16th century, where they were enjoyed by Henry VIII. There are many stories surrounding their origin, most of which involve the recipe being locked away in an iron box to maintain its exclusivity. Nevertheless, a recipe did appear in the second edition of *The Accomplist Cook* by R May, published in 1665, and commercial production of Maids of Honour began in Richmond in 1750, by Thomas Burdekan at his shop in Hill Street. Another old Surrey recipe is Crystal Palace pudding, from a

Mrs Beeton collection published in 1909. This is a jellied custard turned out of a mould and decorated with glace cherries.

*H*askett's Tea & Coffee Shop
A well-cared for old building renowned for its teas

☎ 01306 885833
✉ margaret.garrett@ ukgateway.net

Map ref 3 - TQ14

86 South Street, DORKING, RH4 2EW
🍵 Open Mon-Sat; Tea served 9am-5pm; Closed 25, 26 Dec, 1 Jan; Booking possible; Set tea price(s) £4.95, £5.75; No credit cards; Seats 32; No Smoking; No dogs; Parking 500

*P*oster art from the 1920s and 30s decorates the walls of this tea and coffee shop, but the building itself dates from the late 17th century, and a Grade II listing protects its architectural heritage. A cave with a 220ft well was discovered in the basement, now carefully sealed. A wide variety of tasty dishes is served, like liver and bacon, sausage and mash, and pasta bake, plus breakfasts, sandwiches, omelettes and salads. Afternoon tea is a high spot, with over 20 varieties of tea to revisit or experiment with, as well as 10 different choices of coffees.

The Tea Guild Award of Excellence 2004

RECOMMENDED IN THE AREA
Polesden Lacey; Reigate Priory Museum; Outwood Windmill

*O*atlands Park Hotel ★★★★

Palatial premises in a country setting, but with easy access to the motorway network and airports

☎ 01932 847242
🖷 01932 842252
📧 info@oatlandsparkhotel.com
🌐 www.oatlandsparkhotel.com

Map ref 3 - TQ06

146 Oatlands Drive, WEYBRIDGE,
KT13 9HB
Through Weybridge High Street to top of Monument Hill. Hotel on left.

🍽 Open daily; Tea served 3pm-5pm daily;
No dogs; Set tea price(s) £9.95; Parking 140
🛏 144 Rooms; S £139-£195, D £185-£222

*T*his impressive property occupies the site of a former palace, Oatlands, built by King Henry VIII for Anne of Cleves and subsequently demolished around 1649. The mansion house, which has been destroyed by fire, rebuilt, remodelled and extended over the centuries, is set in extensive grounds complete with tennis courts and a nine-hole golf course. It has been a hotel since 1856, and is easily located for London, the M25, M3 and both Heathrow and Gatwick airports. The galleried lounge provides an opulent setting for afternoon tea, with a glass-domed ceiling, marble pillars and plush seating. Tea can also be taken on the terrace or out on the lawn overlooking the gardens. The comprehensive set meal provides assorted finger sandwiches of smoked salmon, egg mayonnaise, cucumber and cream cheese with chives, freshly baked scones with clotted cream and preserves, and a choice of pastry or cake from the trolley. Alternatives include toasted teacakes and croissants. Parking is provided and children are welcome.

RECOMMENDED IN THE AREA

Wisley RHS Gardens; Brooklands Museum; Hampton Court Palace

Nutfield Priory ★★★★ ◉◉

Victorian country house set in 40 acres of grounds

☎ 01737 824400
📠 01737 823321
✉ nutfield@
handpickedhotels.co.uk
🌐 www.nutfield@
handpicked.co.uk

Map ref 3 - TQ24

Nutfield, REDHILL, RH1 4EL
*M25 junct 6, follow Redhill signs via
Godstone on A25. Hotel 1m on left
after Nutfield Village.*
🍴 Open daily; Tea served 3pm-5pm
daily; Booking possible; Set tea
price(s) £8.50, £15.50, £19.75; Seats
54; Parking 130; No dogs
🛏 60 Rooms; S £120-£165, D £145-£320

There are stunning views over the Surrey countryside from this impressive country house hotel set high on the Nutfield Ridge. Tea is served in the Grand Hall, library or bar, and you can choose a set-price cream tea, afternoon tea or champagne tea. The lounge menu also offers a choice of traditional and speciality sandwiches, such as pressed Mediterranean vegetables glazed with mozzarella served on boccata bread, or minute steak with rocket and Dijon mustard, plus a selection of home-made cakes, pastries, fruit breads, muffins and a cherry and almond tart. During the warmer months you may prefer to sit out on the terrace.

RECOMMENDED IN THE AREA
*Godstone Farm; Hever Castle; Wakehurst
Palace Gardens*

Sussex

Sussex pond pudding is an old-fashioned steamed suet pudding, filling, delicious and very much the ultimate comfort food. To make the pudding the basin is lined with suet pastry and in this case a whole lemon, along with some butter and sugar, is carefully sealed inside the crust before steaming. When you cut into the cooked pudding, the 'pond' of buttery lemon sauce comes flooding out on to the plate until the pudding is swimming in the delightful goo. Alternatively, for Sussex well pudding, dried fruit is included in the suet pastry crust, the pudding basin lined, and the cavity filled with butter and brown sugar before it is covered and steamed. This time, when the cooked pudding is cut into, out gushes a buttery 'well' of sauce to surround the pudding.

Seafood from the Sussex coast is a great teatime treat, with the likes of cod, herrings, mackerel, sprats, plaice, soles, turbot, shrimps, crabs, lobsters, oysters, mussels, cockles, whelks and periwinkles on offer, plus some first rate fish and chips. Locally smoked fish is also a speciality.

*T*he De Vere Grand, Brighton ★★★★

A grand hotel where afternoon tea remains a fashionable social event

☎ 01273 224300
✆ 01273 224321
✉ enquiries@grandbrighton.co.uk
Ⓦ www.grandbrighton.co.uk

Map ref 3 - TQ30

King's Rd, BRIGHTON, BN1 2FW
On seafront between piers, next to Brighton Centre.
☕ Open daily; Tea served 3pm-6pm daily;
Set tea price(s) £13.50; No smoking areas
🛏 200 Rooms; S £170, D £250-£360

*D*ominating the seafront at Brighton, this elaborately adorned Italian Renaissance-style hotel more than lives up to its name. Tea is served daily in the lounge or on the terrace overlooking the English Channel, but please note that tables cannot be booked in advance. The set tea includes a selection of finger sandwiches, freshly baked scones, cakes, French pastries and freshly brewed Indian tea. For a special occasion try the Grand Indulgence – tea as above but with an additional bottle of champagne (for two people).

Parking is available in a public car park to the rear of the hotel. Guide dogs only.

RECOMMENDED IN THE AREA
Royal Pavilion; Brighton Pier; North Laines

---

*S*hepherd's Tea Rooms

Ideal meeting place for tea lovers

☎ 01243 774761

Map ref 3 - SU80

35 Little London, CHICHESTER, PO19 1PL

☕ Open 9.15am-5pm Mon-Fri, 9am-5pm Sat, 10am-4pm Sun;
Tea served all day daily; Closed 25, 26 Dec, 1 Jan, BHs; Booking possible;
Seats 60; No Smoking; Air con

*T*he gentle buzz of contented conversation fills these cosy tea rooms throughout the day until closing time in the late afternoon. Polished wooden floorboards, pale walls and cosy tables create a welcoming atmosphere inside the fine Georgian building. A conservatory-style room at one end allows plenty of light to filter through to the main tea shop, where attentive waitresses serve the home-made food. Salads, sandwiches and at least seven rarebits are among the savoury choices, while early visitors can enjoy a cooked breakfast. The menu offers several loose-leaf teas and popular special blends and traditional afternoon or cream teas along with scrumptious cakes and roulades.

The Tea Guild Award of Excellence 2004.

RECOMMENDED IN THE AREA
Chichester Cathedral; Pallant House Gallery; Mechanical Music & Doll Collection

WALK

West Sussex - Chichester

A fascinating walk combining the ancient treasures of a cathedral city with the delights of the adjacent countryside

After visiting Chichester Cathedral make for the West Door and pass the Bell Tower to reach West Street. Turn right here. Across the road is a converted church, now a pub. The north face of Chichester Cathedral is clearly seen as you head along West Street. On reaching the Market Cross, turn left into North Street and then right immediately beyond the historic Council House into Lion Street. Walk along to St Martin's Square - opposite you at this point is St Mary's Hospital. Turn right and pass the Hole in the Wall pub to reach

East Street. Go straight on into North Pallant and walk along to Pallant House. Keep ahead into South Pallant and follow the road round to the right. Turn left at the next junction, make for the traffic lights and continue south into Southgate. Cross the railway and then swing left to reach the canal basin. Follow the tow path to Poyntz Bridge, dated 1820, and keep ahead to the next bridge which carries the A27 Chichester bypass. Continue to the next footbridge and follow the path to the road. Turn left for a few steps to a stile by

the entrance to a car park. Cross into the field where Chichester's splendid cathedral spire can be seen soaring above the city. Keep the field boundary on your right and make for a footbridge and stile. Continue ahead with lines of trees and bushes on your left. Make for a stile in the field corner and cross the next field, maintaining the same direction. Aim for a stile in the wooded corner and a few steps beyond it you reach the busy A27. Cross over with extreme care to join a footpath opposite. Turn right at the junction and follow the path to the recreation ground. Cross to the far side of the green, looking for Cherry Orchard Road. Turn left at the crossroads into Kingsham Avenue and follow it into Kingsham Road. Turn right at the T-junction, pass the bus station and, on reaching the one-way system, cross over at the lights. Return to the city centre.

DISTANCE: 4.5 miles/7.2km
START/FINISH: Chichester
MAP: OS Explorer 120
TERRAIN : Urban walkways, towpath and field paths
GRADIENT: Flat countryside

*P*avilion Tea Rooms

A period tea room on Eastbourne's seafront

☎ 01323 410374

Map ref 4 - TQ60

Royal Parade, EASTBOURNE,
BN22 7AQ

🍵 Open 10am-4pm in winter, 10am-
5.30pm in summer; Tea served all day;
Closed 25 Dec, 1 Jan; Booking
possible (in winter); Set tea price(s)
£4.85, £7.50; Seats 90 + 40 outside in
summer; No Smoking

RECOMMENDED IN THE AREA
*'How We Lived Then' Museum of Shops &
Social History; Redoubt Fortress &
Museum; Wish Tower Puppet Museum*

A handsome tea rooms, reminiscent of the Victorian/Edwardian era, the Pavilion is located by the Redoubt fortress looking out to sea. Traditionally uniformed waiting staff serve a choice of breakfast dishes, sandwiches, jacket potatoes, and hot dishes such as steak and ale pie, or fillet of salmon with prawn and lobster sauce. Two set teas are offered, a Sussex Cream Tea and a full Pavilion Afternoon Tea with sandwiches, scones and fancy cakes, both served with a pot of Pavilion Blend Tea.

Facilities include a patio tea terrace, sun lounge and souvenir shop, and a pianist plays during summer afternoons and Wednesdays and weekends in the winter. Dogs are not allowed.

*T*he Grand Hotel ★★★★★ ◉◉

An impressive Victorian hotel overlooking the beach and sea

☎ 01323 412345
🅕 01323 412233
🅔 reservations@
   grandeastbourne.com
🅦 www.grandeastbourne.com

Map ref 4 - TQ60

King Edward's Parade,
EASTBOURNE, BN21 4EQ
*On seafront W of Eastbourne, 1m
from railway station.*
🍵 Open daily; Tea served 3pm-6pm
daily; Closed to non-residents 23-26
Dec; Booking required; Set tea
price(s) £12.50-£17.50; Seats 120; No
smoking areas; Parking 60
🛏 152 Rooms; S £135-£400,
D £165-£430

A fternoon tea in the grand style can be taken in the hotel lounges, the Great Hall with its lofty ceiling and marble columns, or on the outdoor pool terrace in summer. For a special treat, tea can be enhanced with a glass of champagne, and on the last Sunday of the month (except June, July and December) the Palm Court Strings play in the Great Hall at tea time. Full

tea comprises a selection of teas, sandwiches, fresh scones with a choice of preserves and clotted cream, fresh strawberries or toasted teacake (according to season), and a selection of freshly made cakes and pastries. No dogs in public areas.

RECOMMENDED IN THE AREA
*Beachy Head & the Seven Sisters; Alfriston village;
Sovereign Harbour marina*

*A*shdown Park Hotel & Country Club ★★★★ ◉◉

A magnificent house and grounds set in the heart of Ashdown Forest

☎ 01342 824988
🖷 01342 826206
✉ reservations@
  ashdownpark.com
🌐 www.ashdownpark.com

Map ref 3 - TQ43

Wych Cross, FOREST ROW, RH18 5JR
*A264 to East Grinstead, then A22 to
Eastbourne, 2m S of Forest Row at
Wych Cross traffic lights. Left to
Hartfield, hotel on right 0.75m.*
☕ Open daily; Tea served Mon-Sat
3.30-5.30pm, Sun 4-5.30pm;
Booking required; Set tea price(s)
£17.50, £23.50; Seats 62 + 50
outside; Parking 200; No dogs
🛏 107 Rooms; S £135-£325,
D £165-£355

*T*he tradition of afternoon tea is proudly maintained at Ashdown Park Hotel, which offers an à la carte tea menu in the relaxed and elegant surroundings of the hotel's drawing rooms or outside on the terrace. Options range from simple tea and crumpets to a Champagne Tea – finger sandwiches, freshly baked scones served warm with clotted cream and a choice of preserves, and a selection of cakes, tea breads and pastries – accompanied by a glass of chilled champagne and fresh strawberries with cream. If you wish to treat someone else to afternoon tea at Ashdown Park, gift certificates are available at reception.

RECOMMENDED IN THE AREA
Sheffield Park Gardens; Hever Castle & Gardens; Penshurst Place

---

*S*outh Lodge Hotel ★★★★ ◉◉◉

Gracious country house setting designed for afternoon tea

☎ 01403 891711
🖷 01403 891766
✉ enquiries@
  southlodgehotel.co.uk
🌐 www.exclusivehotels.co.uk

Map ref 3 - TQ22

Brighton Road, LOWER BEEDING,
RH13 6PS
*On A23 left onto B2110. Right through
Handcross to A281 junct. Left and
hotel on right.*
☕ Open daily; Tea served 3pm;
Booking possible; Set tea price(s)
£8.50, £15.00; Seats 30 + 70 outside;
Air con; Parking 100
🛏 39 Rooms; S £150, D £195-£380

*H*ome-made afternoon tea served on the terrace overlooking the South Downs – there can be few experiences more English, or more delightful. South Lodge is an exclusive country house hotel, where Victorian splendours are still apparent in the reception rooms, and hospitality is warm and discreet. Freshly-brewed tea and coffee are served on their own, or to accompany cream teas or the full afternoon tea of finger sandwiches, scones, teacakes and pastries. The lounge and terrace menu also tempts with cocktails, hot sandwiches, light lunches and desserts.

RECOMMENDED IN THE AREA
Leonardslee Gardens; Parham House & Gardens; Borde Hill Garden

*T*he Tea Tree Tea Rooms

A pretty tea shop in medieval Winchelsea, serving tasty teas and meals, where gifts are also on sale

☎ 01797 226102   ✆ 01797 229672
✉ theteatree@btconnect.com   ⊛ www.the-tea-tree.co.uk

Map ref 4 - TQ91

12 High Street, WINCHELSEA, TN36 4EA
On A259 between Hastings & Rye. In centre of town beyond town gate.
☕ Open 10am-5pm (6pm weekends & BHs); Tea served all day; Closed Tues & Jan; Set tea price(s) fr £4.75 - £15; Seats 66 (incl garden); No Smoking; No Dogs

RECOMMENDED IN THE AREA
Winchelsea Town Museum;
Rye Harbour Nature Reserve &
Camber Castle; Rye Castle Museum,
Winchelsea Ancient Monuments

*I*n the heart of 1066 country close to Rye, the historic Cinque Port of Winchelsea plays host to this welcoming tea shop located close to the medieval town gate. The quaint old double-fronted shop dates from the 15th century, and boasts those essential adjuncts of the period – exposed beams and an inglenook fireplace. Inside the smart tea room and adjoining conservatory, dark wood furniture and gaily-coloured checked tablecloths are an irresistible invitation to take a seat and study the menu; in warmer weather, the courtyard garden is equally inviting. The choice includes a range of home-cooked meals, sandwiches, salads, ploughman's and baguettes, with the tea shop's hallmark giant meringues and freshly-baked cakes always making an appearance. Many visitors come especially for afternoon tea, when an individual pot of the chosen loose-leaf is served with sandwiches, scones with strawberry jam and cream, and cakes. The gift shop, selling collectables such as teapots, mugs and tea sets, plus teas, coffees, jams, chutneys, honeys and greetings cards is also popular.

WALK

East Sussex - Winchelsea

Explore one of the old Cinque Ports before following a historic line of defence

With Winchelsea's New Inn on your left and the ruined St Thomas's Church on the right, follow the road round the right-hand bend. Head down to Strand Gate and then follow the road to the junction with the A259. Turn right and follow the pavement along here. When the road bends left, turn right at the sign for Winchelsea Beach. Cross the Royal Military Canal and turn immediately right. Follow the towpath, cross a stile and avoid a concrete footbridge. Eventually the canal begins to curve left. Look for a stile and galvanised gate here. Turn

right a few paces beyond it at the footbridge. Cross a second footbridge over a ditch and make for a stile. Pass the birdwatching hide and continue along the path, making for the next footbridge. Cross it, veer right and then follow the path as it curves left through the reedbeds. Begin a moderate climb and head towards a house. Keep to the left of it and follow the path through the trees. Join a drive, pass Ashes Farm and look for a stile on the left. Go diagonally across the field to a stile, then turn right for a few paces to two more stiles. Skirt the field to

the next stile and exit to the road. Keep right here, signposted 'Winchelsea', and soon you pass below a hilltop windmill. Go straight ahead over a stile when the lane bends left and cross the field. Look for a stile and keep alongside some trees to the next stile. Continue ahead, pass an old pillbox and head down the gentle field slope to the road. Turn right for a few paces to a stile on the left. Cross it and swing right, following the 1066 Country Walk to the next stile. Keep to the right of Wickham Manor and look for a stile in the far boundary. Cross the drive to a stile and keep ahead across the fields. Make for a stile and gate in the bottom left corner and follow the 1066 Country Walk waymarks. The path veers over to the right to two stiles. Turn left and begin a moderate ascent to a stone stile. Turn right at the road, follow it round to the left and return to the centre of Winchelsea.

DISTANCE: 4.5 miles/7.2km
START/FINISH: Winchelsea
MAP: OS Explorer 124
TERRAIN : Mixture of marshland and undulating farmland
GRADIENT: Moderate climbing

Speciality Teas:
• take their name from the plantation on which they are grown
(usually referred to as single estate or single source teas)
• come from a particular area or country
• are blended for a particular time of day or occasion
• are blends to which flower, fruit, herb or spice flavourings have been added.

India, South Africa and Indonesia

Teas from India
Assam

The hot and steamy conditions of the Brahmaputra River Valley in Assam in north-east India produce black teas that give a full-bodied, rich, dark liquor that enjoys a smooth, malty flavour. Assam is an ideal breakfast tea, and is readily available in Britain, although it is harder to find the subtler single-source teas that come from named estates. Use milk to taste.

Darjeeling

Grown in the Himalayan mountains, several thousand feet above sea level, Darjeeling is known as the champagne of teas. The cold winters and hot summers give a concentrated, slightly astringent flavour that is prized all over the world. Drink without milk.

Nilgiri

The black teas from Nilgiri hills in the south of India are bright, fruity and flavoursome and are often blended with lighter teas to add strength and interest.

Teas from Kenya

You probably had some Kenyan tea this morning. Britain buys around 50% of its teas from Kenya, as the strong rich flavour and dark, coppery infusion is ideal for the blends that go into everyday teabags. Best drunk with milk, the British way.

Tea from South Africa
Zulu Tea

A black tea from Kwazulu, this is the only South African tea to be exported for international consumption. The flavour is lively and strong and is best drunk with milk.

Teas from Indonesia

Indonesian black teas are light and flavoursome. Most are sold for blending purposes as and are a major source of foreign currency for Indonesia. It is possible to buy some single estate Indonesian teas and these are very refreshing drunk without milk but perhaps with a slice of lemon.

Warwickshire

Warwickshire Truckle cheese has been made to the same recipe for 75 years by Fowlers of Earlswood in Warwickshire. The company also produces an oak-smoked version, a handmade blue cheese (Fowlers Forest Blue) and the Fowlers Warwickshire range of cheeses, flavoured with the likes of garlic and parsley, chilli, chive and onion, and cracked black pepper.
Warwick rarebit – a variation on Welsh rarebit – is a happy combination of toast topped with a sauce made from Warwickshire Truckle and one of Warwickshire's real ales.
Hand-made sausages are also a speciality in the county, and

farmers' markets at Stratford-Upon-Avon, Kenilworth, Warwick, Royal Leamington Spa, Rugby, Southam and Coleshill are great places to pick up local fare.

Stratford Manor ★★★★

Welcoming modern hotel serving agreeable teas

☎ 01789 731173
📠 01789 731131
✉ stratfordmanor@marstonhotels.com
🌐 www.marstonhotels.com

Map ref 3 - SP25

Warwick Road,
STRATFORD-UPON-AVON,
CV37 0PY
3m N of town centre on A439 in direction of Warwick, or from M40 junct 15, A439 to Stratford-upon-Avon, hotel 2m on left.
Open daily; Tea served all day; Closed 25-Dec; Booking possible; Set tea price(s) £9.50; Seats 50; Air con; No dogs; Parking 200;
104 Rooms; S £108, D £130

Lovely gardens and the countryside beyond are a fine setting for this modern hotel close to the centre of Stratford-uon-Avon. With the town's delights so near at hand, and the rest of Warwickshire on the doorstep, this is an ideal centre for touring the area. Leisure facilities are provided for overnight visitors, with two all-weather tennis courts and a heated indoor pool just the thing for those seeking to relax through exercise. For the perfect pick-me-up you can head for the cocktail bar and order tea: speciality sandwiches, scones, cakes and Danish pastries are all on the menu, served with a fine pot of tea.

RECOMMENDED IN THE AREA
Shakespeare's Birthplace; Hall's Croft; Butterfly Farm

Stratford Victoria ★★★★ ◉

Enjoy a choice of teas in perfect comfort

☎ 01789 271000
🖷 01789 271001
✉ stratfordvictoria@
   marstonhotels.com
🌐 www.marstonhotels.com

Map ref 3 - SP25

Arden Street,
STRATFORD-UPON-AVON,
CV37 6QQ
*A439 into Stratford, follow A3400
Birmingham, at traffic light junct left
into Arden St, hotel 150yds on right.*
♨ Open daily; Tea served all day;
Closed 25-Dec; Booking possible; Set
tea price(s) £9.50; Seats 40; No dogs;
Parking 200
🛏 102 Rooms; S £99, D £125

Attractive modern hotel with interesting architectural features and a red brick façade. The centre of historic Stratford is just a short walk away, and the hotel has its own gardens for guests to relax in. Other notable features are the mini-gym for a quick workout, a whirlpool spa and a beauty salon. For lovers of the afternoon tea ritual there is a set choice or a pick-your-own version. Finger sandwiches, scones with preserves an cream, and cakes with a pot of your favourite fine tea, coffe or chocolate are served ensemble, or you can choose you own sandwiches, Danish pastries, or fruit cakes from th menu.

RECOMMENDED IN THE AREA

The Teddy Bear Museum; New Place/Nash's House; Anne Hathaway's Cottage

Wiltshire

Wiltshire has been at the centre of the bacon industry since the 18th century when many pigs were imported from Ireland to Bristol and were herded from the port along the drove roads to London. Calne was a regular resting point on the way, and so was assured a regular supply of pigs for curing. The traditional Wiltshire cure, dating back 300 years, produces a mildly flavoured, low-salt ham, ideal for sandwiches. The cooling of the meat using ice was introduced to Calne in 1856, enabling the Wiltshire cure to be applied on a large scale, providing bacon, ham and gammon for the whole country and for the export market.

The ever-popular lardy cake originally comes from Wiltshire; a bread dough stuffed with as much lard, fruit and sugar as the fancy takes the baker.

The Bridge Tea Rooms

An award-winning tea shop where top quality teas are elegantly served in fine bone china cups

☎ 01225 865537

Map ref 2 - ST76

24a Bridge Street, BRADFORD ON AVON, BA15 1BY
Close to Saxon bridge.

Open Mon-Fri 9.30am-5pm, Sat 9.30am-5.30pm, Sun 12-5.30pm; Tea served all day; Closed 25 & 26 Dec; Booking possible; Set tea price(s) £6.95-£16.95; No credit cards; Seats 48; No Smoking; No Dogs

The afternoon ritual of serving tea has been developed to a fine art here, and is so accomplished that the Bridge Tea Rooms has been recognized as excellent by the prestigious Tea Guild. Put aside any notions of dangling a tea bag in a mug, and think instead of delicate Royal Doulton china, the finest leaf teas, and friendly staff in Victorian costumes serving home-made cakes, pastries and sandwiches. Housed in a former blacksmith's cottage dating from 1675, the Bridge Tea Rooms positively oozes atmosphere, and the classical music playing gently in the background sets a tranquil tone. Interesting light meals are also served throughout the day (every day except Christmas and Boxing Day!), but the famous Bridge Cream Tea is the main attraction here: expect large scones topped with Devonshire clotted cream and strawberry preserve, and a pot of one of 26 fine loose leaf teas presented to perfection in a beautiful teapot. Souvenir books and postcards are on sale.

The Tea Guild Award of Excellence 2004.

RECOMMENDED IN THE AREA

Saxon church, Tithe barn (c.1341); The Courts, Holt; Westwood Manor; Great Chalfield Manor; City of Bath

*J*acqueline's Restaurant & Tea Rooms

Excellent range of food and speciality teas

☎ 01985 217373
✉ jacquelinesrestaurant@
hotmail.com

Map ref 2 - ST84

28 High Street, WARMINSTER, BA12 9AF

🍵 Open Mon-Sat; Tea served all day;
Booking possible; Set tea price(s) £3.65 (with
coffee £3.95), £5.65 (with coffee £5.95);
Seats 40; No Smoking

*Q*uality organic food, cooked from fresh loca
produce wherever possible, is the key to th
success of this popular tea room. Located in th
centre of the old Wiltshire town, it is no surprise tha
it has been the winner of several tea awards
Owners Jacqui and Mark serve a wide range of foo
throughout the day, from cooked breakfasts t
lunches such as steak baguette with onions, bake
potato with smoked salmon and cream cheese, an
prawn omelette. For the sweettoothed, there ar
home-made cakes and desserts, cream teas, an
afternoon tea, all served with a speciality tea, or
herbal or fruit variety.

RECOMMENDED IN THE AREA

*Longleat House & Safari Park; Stourton House
Flower Gardens; Stourhead House & Gardens*

Yorkshire

Yorkshire has a rich heritage of traditional recipes, probably the best known of which is the Yorkshire pudding. A batter-based dish, rising to light, golden heights, Yorkshire pudding appears in many guises these days, from plate-sized filled Yorkshire pudding, through toad in the hole with sausages cooked in with the batter, to tiny and sophisticated canapés.

Yorkshire is another northern oat-growing area, where spicy, treacly, teatime treats include delicious sticky parkin, gingerbreads and brandy snaps.

Parkin is also a customary Bonfire Night cake. Yorkshire teacakes are yeasted buns made with currants and candied peel and given a sweet sticky glaze. To serve, they should be split, toasted and laden with butter.

Wensleydale cheese is made in the area around Hawes in Wensleydale. White Wensleydale, using finely cut, lightly pressed curd, takes only three weeks to ripen and has a mild flavour and crumbly texture. Blue veined Wensleydale, far more pungent, takes six months to mature and

is not unlike blue Stilton. White Wensleydale cheese is traditionally eaten with apple pie and fruitcake.

York ham is mild, lean and ideal for sandwiches. It is a more expensive product than other hams because of the special process of its preparation, which takes several months.

What is Yorkshire famous for?

Breathtaking scenery, cricket and Yorkshire Tea! For three generations our family business here in Yorkshire has been blending tea for our Bettys Tea Rooms. Once we started putting our tea into packets, word quickly spread beyond the borders of Yorkshire to the rest of the country, and Yorkshire Tea was born.

Our tea tasters sample hundreds of teas every week, just to find the few good enough to give Yorkshire Tea its lovely, rich taste and distinctive briskness. We even take the time and trouble to blend our tea to suit your water, whether it's hard or soft.

The home of Yorkshire Tea has bee captured in watercolours by artist Lizz Sanders for our new box. We hope it w find a place on your kitchen shelf to remi you of Yorkshire and a lovely cup of tea.

For a free sample write to us Yorkshire Tea, PO Box 137, Harroga HG2 7UJ or visit our website www.yorkshiretea.co.uk.

...a lovely cup of tea

*T*he Georgian Tea Rooms

Quintessentially English tea rooms in one of the country's most complete Georgian streets

☎ 01262 608600
✉ GADandy@aol.com

Map ref 8 - TA26

56 High Street, Old Town, BRIDLINGTON, East Riding of Yorkshire, YO16 4QA

☕ Open Mon-Sat 10am-5pm, Sun 10am-3pm; Tea served all day; Closed 2 weeks Christmas & New Year; Booking possible; No credit cards; Seats 39 + 24 outside; No smoking areas

A delightfully refreshing discovery in Bridlington's historic Old Town, the Georgian Tea Rooms occupies the ground floor of a Grade II listed building, and enhances its period charm with beautifully kept antique furniture. The proprietors, Diane Davison and her brother David Rothwell painstakingly restored the building some five years ago, and on the two floors above they have showrooms filled with antiques, collectables and objets d'art, where customers are sure to enjoy browsing. The patio and large garden to the rear, with its antique fountain, is a great attraction in fine weather, with seating for a further couple of dozen people. The menu offers home-cooked food, freshly prepared from locally-supplied ingredients. Particular favourites are the selection of home-made quiches, cakes and pastries, although the food options range through cooked breakfasts, light lunches, sandwiches and ices, with daily specials extending from tasty savouries to additional cakes. Family functions can also be catered for. No dogs except guide dogs.

The Tea Guild Award of Excellence 2004.

RECOMMENDED IN THE AREA

Heritage Coast of Flamborough Head;
Bempton Cliffs RSPB Bird Colony;
Burton Agnes Elizabethan Hall

*A*ldwark Manor ★★★★ ◉◉

19th-century mansion with inbuilt style

☎ 01347 838146
🖷 01347 838867
✉ aldwark@marstonhotels.com
🌐 www.marstonhotels.com

Map ref 8 - SE46

ALDWARK, North Yorkshire,
YO61 1UF
*A1/A59 towards Green Hammerton,
then B6265 Little Ouseburn. Follow
signs for Aldwark Bridge/Manor. A19
through Linton on Ouse.*
☕ Open daily; Tea served 2pm-
4.30pm; Closed 25-Dec; Booking
possible; Set tea price(s) £4.95, £9.95
Seats 60; No Smoking; Air con; No
dogs; Parking 200
🛏 60 Rooms; S £75, D £125

*T*his large Victorian manor is gloriously set in 100 acres of natural parkland with the River Ure flowing through. The grounds feature a challenging 18-hole golf course which surrounds the rambling hotel building, and there is a leisure centre with a heated swimming pool, spa, gym, steam room, massage rooms and beauty salons. Cossetting of a very different kind comes in the form of afternoon tea served in the gracious surroundings of the Terrace Bar. You can give yourself a treat with scones, clotted cream, classy preserves, finger sandwiches, and you choice of tea from a speciality range.

RECOMMENDED IN THE AREA
York City Art Gallery; National Railway Museum; Fairfax House

*C*larks Café

Family-run bakery and café halfway between York and Thirsk

☎ 01347 821285

Map ref 8 - SE57

195 Long Street, EASINGWOLD,
North Yorkshire, YO6 3JB
☕ Open Mon-Sat; Tea served 8am-
4.30pm (4 on Sat); Closed Sun & BHs;
No credit cards; Seats 30;
No Smoking

*C*larks was established by the proprietor's mother in 1925, who began by selling tea and home-baked scones to road repair men from Middlesborough. The café's display of colourful canal-ware reflects Gerald and Judy Clark's enthusiasm for narrow boats, and there's also a pretty garden with outside seating. Everything is made on the premises, and house specialities are the all-day breakfast, brunch, ploughman's/gamekeeper's lunch, and the set afternoon or cream tea. Other options range from chip butty, omelettes and sandwiches to teatime treats such as sausage rolls, teacakes, vanilla slice and fruitcake serve with Wensleydale cheese. The Clarks have a second t room in the town centre. Guide dogs only. Parking provide

RECOMMENDED IN THE AREA
City of York; North York Moors; Castle Howard

*C*larks Tearooms

The Clarks' second tea room in town-centre Easingwold

☎ 01347 823143

Map ref 8 - SE57

Market Place, EASINGWOLD, North Yorkshire, YO6 3AG
☕ Open Mon-Sat; Tea served 10am-5pm; Closed Sun & BHs; No credit cards; Seats 40; No Smoking

RECOMMENDED IN THE AREA
City of York, North York Moors, Castle Howard

*T*he original family bakery and café, situated on the edge of town, is complemented by this conveniently located tea room in Easingwold's Market Place. The menus are similar, with house specialities such as set afternoon tea, ploughman's/gamekeeper's lunch and cream tea, supplemented by daily specials from the blackboard. Enduringly popular are the range of sandwiches and toasties, light meals, pork pies, sausage rolls and home-made cakes. Local delicacies include traditional Yorkshire fruitcake with Wensleydale cheese, Yorkshire curd tart, and Clark's home-made toasted tea loaf. Home bakery products and pictures of the local area are also available to buy. Guide dogs only. Free parking in town centre.

*B*ettys Café Tea Rooms, Harrogate

First of the five Bettys, opened in 1919

☎ 01423 877300
✆ 01423 877307
ⓦ www.bettysandtaylors.co.uk

Map ref 7 - SE35

1 Parliament Square, HARROGATE, North Yorkshire, HG1 2QU
☕ Open 9am-9pm daily; Tea served all day; Closed 25 & 26 Dec, 1 Jan; Set tea price(s) £5.65, £10.00; Seats 130; No Smoking; Air con

*W*hen young confectioner Frederick Belmont travelled from Switzerland to find his fortune he came to Harrogate accidentally – by catching the wrong train. He liked the place well enough to stay, married a local lass and opened the first Bettys. Today's unique Swiss/Yorkshire menu continues to reflect the heritage of the family business. Taylors of Harrogate is a sister company, importing and blending all the teas served, and each of the tea rooms has a shop selling teas, coffees, speciality breads, cakes, patisserie and chocolates, all hand made at Bettys Craft Bakery. Cookery courses are also available at Bettys Cookery School, also in Harrogate. Children welcome; guide dogs only.

The Tea Guild Award of Excellence 2004.

RECOMMENDED IN THE AREA
Fountains Abbey; The Royal Pump Room Museum; RHS Garden at Harlow Carr

*B*ettys Café Tea Rooms, Ilkley

A strikingly attractive tea room on the tree-lined Grove

☎ 01943 608029
🖷 01943 816723
🌐 www.bettysandtaylors.co.uk

Map ref 7 - SE24

32-34 The Grove, ILKLEY,
West Yorkshire, YO1 2QP
☕ Open 9am-5.30pm daily; Tea
served all day; Closed 25 & 26 Dec, 1
Jan; Set tea price(s) £5.65, £10.00;
Seats 54; No smoking; Air con

*O*ne of the five famous Bettys, the Ilkley incarnation has a wrought-iron canopy and an extensive tea and coffee counter stacked with antique tea caddies. Other notable features are the specially commissioned stained glass windows, depicting wild flowers from Ilkley Moor, and the large teapot collection. The tea room is a favourite with ramblers, tired, hungry and thirsty from a tramp across the moors. The guiding principle of Bettys' founder, Frederick Belmont, was that 'if we want things just right we have to make them ourselves', and Bettys Bakery still makes all the cakes, pastries, chocolates, breads and scones serve in the tea rooms. Children welcome; guide dogs only.

The Tea Guild Award of Excellence 2004.

RECOMMENDED IN THE AREA
Ilkley Moor; Haworth Parsonage; National Museum of Photography, Film & Television

*B*ettys Café Tea Rooms, Northallerton

The most northerly of the five Bettys tea rooms

☎ 01609 775154
🖷 01609 777552
🌐 www.bettysandtaylors.co.uk

Map ref 8 - SE39

188 High Street, NORTHALLERTON,
North Yorkshire, DL7 8LF

☕ Open Mon-Sat 9am-5.30pm, Sun
10am-5.30pm; Tea served all day;
Closed 25 & 26 Dec, 1 Jan; Set tea
price(s) £5.65, £10.00; Seats 58; No
Smoking; Air con

RECOMMENDED IN THE AREA
North York Moors; Flamingo Land; Rievaulx Abbey

*T*he Northallerton branch of Bettys is a sunny golden room, intimate in scale, decorated with art deco mirrors and antique teapots. Two set teas are offered: a Yorkshire Cream Tea with two sultana scones, butter, strawberry preserve and Yorkshire clotted cream, or the Bettys Traditional Afternoon Tea with a choice of sandwich, a sultana scone with butter, preserve and cream, followed by a choice of Yorkshire curd tart or chocolate éclair. In both cases the tea in the pot is Bettys Tea Roo Blend of top class African and Assam tea Children are welcome and good facilities a provided to keep them fed, cleane changed and entertained. Guide dogs on

The Tea Guild Award of Excellence 200

WALK

Through Viking York

The Jorvik Viking Centre, located on the site of the Coppergate excavations in York, vividly recreates a 9th-century settlement whose winding streets are still walked today

JORVIK VIKING CENTRE

From the car park, turn right, then right again at the trafficlights. Go through Micklegate Bar. Take the next right (Priory Street). At the end, turn left, pass the church, then turn right along Bishophill Senior. Opposite the Golden Ball pub, turn left down Carr's Lane. At the bottom, turn right along Skeldergate, keeping left at the fork. Go under Skeldergate Bridge. Continue along the river bank and cross the Millennium Bridge. Go by the white gate and walk up Maple Grove to Fulford

Road. Turn left towards the city centre. Walk up Piccadilly between the Travelodge and medieval tower (Fishergate Postern). After the mini-roundabout, turn left along a glazed passage signed Castle Area, Jorvik Viking Centre. Go right, through glass doors, and out into St Mary's Square. The Viking Centre is diagonally right.

After your visit, continue from the square up the slope between the Viking Centre and Boots store. At the top of the slope, turn right. At the traffic-lights, go straight on, and after the Marks and Spencer store turn left up the Shambles. At the top, turn right. Go half-right across King's Square into

Goodramgate. Where the road bends right, turn left and follow the road, passing between York Minster and St Michael-le-Belfrey Church. Continue up High Petergate and through Bootham Bar.
Cross at the lights and go up Bootham. Turn left down Marygate by the circular tower. Just beyond the church, go left through the archway. Continue ahead to leave the gardens by the lodge. Cross and keep ahead down Lendal, and straight on to the trafficlights by St Michael's Church. Turn right, cross Ouse Bridge, go through two more sets of trafficlights and up Micklegate. Pass through Micklegate Bar. Turn left back to the car park.

DISTANCE: 5.25 miles (8.4km)
START/FINISH: Viking Centre car park
MAP: OS Explorer 290
PATHS: city pavements
TERRAIN : City pavements and riverside
GRADIENT: Level except for one climb up Micklegate

E Botham & Sons

Famous tea rooms specialising in Victorian recipes and fine teas

☎ 01947 602823
📠 01947 820269
✉ sales@botham.co.uk
🌐 www.botham.co.uk

Map ref 8 - NZ91

35/39 Skinner Street, WHITBY, North Yorkshire, YO21 3AH
🍵 Open 9am-4.30pm; Tea served all day; Closed Sun & Mon (Sep-May), Sun (Jun-Aug) 25, 26 Dec, 1 Jan, some BHs; Booking possible; Set tea price(s) £2.80. £5.65; Seats 100; No Smoking

*T*he invitation to take tea at Botham's is an irresistible one involving wonderful cakes and pastries made from Victorian recipes, and a huge range of rare and fine teas. Botham's was established in 1865 by Elizabeth Botham and is still run by her great-grandchildren. The first-floor tea-rooms offer scones and teabreads, cream teas and toasts, special lunches such as quiche and chips, jacket potatoes, salads and sandwiches. Afternoon tea comes with a pot of your choice: you'll find China Yunnan, Java Gunpowder and Darjeeling First Flush Bannockburn, or if your taste is for coffee, a variety of classic blends. No dogs.

The Tea Guild Award of Excellence 2004.

RECOMMENDED IN THE AREA
Whitby Abbey; Danby Moors Centre; Sea Life & Marine Sanctuary

---

*B*ettys Café Tea Rooms, York

Bettys York flagship café in the heart of the city

☎ 01904 659142
📠 01904 627050
🌐 www.bettysandtaylors.co.uk

Map ref 8 - SE65

6-8 St Helen's Square, YORK, North Yorkshire, YO1 8QP
🍵 Open 9am-9pm; Tea served all day; Closed 25 & 26 Dec, 1 Jan; Set tea price(s) £5.85 (cream tea), £10.25 (afternoon tea); Seats 213; No Smoking; Air con

RECOMMENDED IN THE AREA
York Minster; Castle Howard; York Dungeon

*I*n 1936 Frederick Belmont, Bettys founder, travelled on the maiden voyage of the Queen Mary, during which time he was planning a new café in York. The luxury liner provided the required inspiration, and the ship's interior designers were commissioned to recreate the magnificent panelling, pillars and mirrors in the elegant new premises. Favourite dishes encompass Swiss rösti, Alpine macaroni, Masham sausages and Yorkshire Rarebit, plus a fine selection of cakes, patisserie and desserts. Children have always been welcome, and there's a 'Little Rascals' menu, books, toys organic baby food and both gents' and ladies' baby-changing facilities. A café pianist enhances the atmosphere during the evenings. Guide dogs only.

The Tea Guild Award of Excellence 200

*B*ullivant of York

All-day home-cooked fare in a city centre location

☎ 01904 671311

Map ref 8 - SE65

15 Blake Street, YORK,
North Yorkshire, YO1 2QJ

☕ Open Mon-Fri 9.30am-5pm, Sat
9am-5pm; Tea served all day; Closed
Sun, 24-26 Dec; Booking possible;
Set tea price(s) £3.75, £4.25;
Seats 43 + 14 outside;
No smoking areas

RECOMMENDED IN THE AREA
*York Minster; The ARC ('hands-on'
archaeological museum); Fairfax House*

A good choice of teas, coffees and herbal infusions is
available at this friendly tea room, which has fine
weather seating in the courtyard outside. The menu lists an
extensive selection of meals, sandwiches and snacks
prepared to order, plus an enticing range of home-made
desserts. Set teas include a traditional high tea, cream tea
and the speciality Chocolate Heaven – chocolate chip
scone with Yorkshire clotted cream and luxury praline

chocolate spread served with hot
chocolate. The high tea offers baked beans
on toast or boiled egg with toasted soldiers
as an alternative to sandwiches. Home
made jams and chutneys are available to
buy.

Guide dogs only.

*L*ittle Bettys

A listed building in medieval Stonegate close to the Minster

☎ 01904 622865
🖷 01904 640348
🌐 www.bettysandtaylors.co.uk

Map ref 8 - SE65

46 Stonegate, YORK, North Yorkshire,
YO1 8AS
☕ Open 10am-5.30pm Sun-Fri, 9am-
5.30pm Sat; Tea served all day;
Closed 25 & 26 Dec, 1 Jan; Set tea price(s)
£5.65, £10.00; Seats 65; No Smoking; Air con

*T*here are five versions of Bettys, two of them in York, and this is the smallest of all. The café is reached via a flight of winding stairs and has a delightful interior characterised by wooden beams and roaring fires. Hot dishes, speciality sandwiches and an extensive range of cakes and patisserie are served, with the Yorkshire Fat Rascal as a house speciality – a large fruity scone with citrus peel, almonds and cherries. Teas are supplied by Bettys' sister company, family tea merchants Taylors of Harrogate, including some UK exclusives. Bettys is famously family-friendly, and children are made particularly welcome. Guide dogs only.

RECOMMENDED IN THE AREA
York Minster; Jorvik Viking Centre; National Railway Museum

The Tea Guild Award of Excellence 2004.

---

*J*udges Country House Hotel ★★★ ⑩⑩⑩

Gracious mansion set in landscaped grounds

☎ 01642 789000
🖷 01642 782878
✉ enquiries@judgeshotel.co.uk
🌐 www.judgeshotel.co.uk

Map ref 8 - NZ41

Kirklevington Hall, YARM, North
Yorkshire, TS15 9LW
1.5m from A19. At A67 junct, follow Yarm road, hotel on left.
☕ Open daily; Tea served 2.30pm-
5pm; Booking possible; Set tea
price(s) £10.50, £15.50; Seats 40;
Parking 102
🛏 21 Rooms; S £104-£130,
D £120-£170

*F*ormerly lodgings for local circuit judges – hence the name – the house has been extensively renovated to create stylish accommodation. The hotel prides itself on all the little extras it offers to its guests, even extending to goldfish in the rooms. Full afternoon tea, served in the lounge, is an event that has been known to last until the early evening. It includes a selection of finger and open sandwiches, freshly baked plain and fruit warm scones served with three preserves and Devonshire clotted cream, home-made pastries from the French patissier's platter, Victoria sponge and warm biscuits. A glass of rosé or brut champagne is an optional extra. Guide dogs only.

RECOMMENDED IN THE AREA
Preston Park; Yarm; Captain Cook's Museum

WHERE THE DALES MEET THE ALPS

Few visitors to Harrogate fail to visit Bettys Café Tea Rooms. Founded in 1919 by Frederick Belmont, a Swiss Confectioner, Bettys reputation for old-fashioned hospitality, mouth-watering cakes, and award-winning cups of tea has made it world famous.

More than eighty years later, Bettys is still a family business owned by the descendants of Frederick Belmont. Bettys is remarkably self-sufficient and remains true to the founder's principle that. "If you want something just right, you have to do it yourself." All the cakes, breads, and chocolates served at Bettys are made by hand at Bettys Craft Bakery. The Sister company, family tea merchants Taylors of Harrogate, imports and blends an extensive range of teas and coffees.

Every effort is still made today to ensure that your visit to Bettys is a memorable one. Each evening a Café Pianist adds to the intimate atmosphere and, as always, you'll be made welcome whether it's for a quick coffee or a full supper with Swiss wine. There's also a special 'Little Rascals' menu, and everything you need to make your visit with younger guests as easy as possible.

Bettys Café Tea Rooms can be found in Harrogate, York, Ilkley, and Northallerton. There is also Little Bettys on Stonegate in York, not far from York Minster.

For more information on Bettys, Bettys Cookery School, and Bettys by Post, please visit www.bettysandtaylors.co.uk

Buying, Storing and Brewing Tea

When you buy packaged tea, make sure that packets and tins are undamaged and that any wrapping is intact. It is important that the tea has been kept in air-tight conditions in order to preserve flavour and quality.

When buying loose-leaf tea, it is worth remembering that tea keeps best at the retailer's shop when stored in large canisters that have air-tight lids with a strong seal. Tea should not be stored in glass, and is best in cool, dry conditions.

The leaf should look dry and even and all the pieces of leaf should be approximately the same size. An uneven blend that has leaves of varying particle size can cause problems when brewing as the different sized pieces of leaf will release their flavour and colour at different rates, thereby giving an unbalanced overall flavour and quality.

At home, always store leaf and bagged tea in an air-tight container with a tightly-fitting lid and keep in a cool dry place away from other strong flavours and smells, as tea easily absorbs other flavours.

Brewing a good cup of tea

• Always use good quality loose leaf or bagged tea

• Always fill the kettle with freshly drawn cold water

• When brewing black and oolong teas, allow the water to reach boiling point before pouring on to the leaves

• When brewing green tea, boil the water and then allow it to cool slightly before pouring on to the leaves

• Measure the tea carefully into the pot: use one tea bag or one rounded teaspoon of loose tea for each cup to be served

• Allow the tea to brew for the correct number of minutes. Small leafed black tea normally needs 2-3 minutes; larger leafed black tea needs 3-5 minutes; oolong teas need 5-7 minutes; green teas need 1-3 minutes. Where possible, follow instructions on packets or test each tea to find the number of minutes that suits you.

Scotland

Oats were long a staple of the Scottish diet and this is reflected in foods still widely served today, like Scottish oatcakes, which are crisp biscuits, good with cheese or sweet preserves, and cranachan, a delicious mixture of toasted oatmeal, cream and soft fruit like raspberries and strawberries, which are grown in abundance in Scotland. Whisky, Scottish liqueurs and heather honey are frequently added to dishes, including fruitcakes, desserts and tablet to impart a Scottish flavour. Tablet is a sweetie made from sugar, butter and condensed milk, a bit like fudge but slightly harder. Scotland has a fabulous range of tea breads, cakes and biscuits. Among these are Scots pancakes, a batter mix fried on a griddle and served with butter, and the satisfying potato scone. Bannocks are a kind of oat-based scone cooked on a griddle, but there are some wide variations. Selkirk bannock is a sweet fruit bread, cooked as a loaf and served sliced with butter, while Pitcaithy bannock is more like a shortbread with almonds and candied peel. Scotland is renowned for its delicious shortbread, and in some remote parts of the country it served as bride's cake. As the bride entered her new home, the decorated shortbread would be broken over her head and the pieces distributed among her friends. The classic Scottish fruitcake, Dundee cake, is rich and buttery, decorated with circles of blanched almonds, while black bun is traditional Hogmanay fare, a mixture of fruit and spices cooked as a loaf in a pastry casing. Aberdeen butteries are bread rolls with a very high butter content, a little like croissants in some respects, and are generally available all over Aberdeenshire. Favourite savouries include smoked salmon, Arbroath smokies (lightly smoked haddock generally flaked and served with a creamy sauce), and Forfar bridies, which are meat pies a bit like Cornish pasties in appearance.

The Coach House Coffee Shop

A village coffee shop on the western shore of Loch Lomond

☎ 01436 860341
🖷 01436 860336
✉ enquiries@
  lochlomondtrading.com
🌐 www.lochlomondtrading.com

Map ref 9 - NS39

LUSS, Argyll & Bute, G83 8NN
☕ Open daily; Tea served 10am-5pm
daily; Booking possible; Seats 150;
No Smoking

*L*uss provides the delightful setting for Gary and Rowena Groves' café/gift shop, where you are likely to be welcomed by a log fire, Gaelic music and a traditionally kilted proprietor. It is called a coffee shop, but has plenty to offer the tea connoisseur. Light meals and snacks with a Scottish flavour are served in generous portions, and home-made soup, home-baked rolls and home-produced free range eggs are featured. Speciality fruitcakes are laced with malt whisky or baked with ale and studded with crystallised ginger. Goods available for sale include teas, coffees, teapots, confectionary and cakes. Parking is available in the main village car park.

The Tea Guild Award of Excellence 2004.

RECOMMENDED IN THE AREA
Loch Lomond Cruises; Luss Glen; Ben Lomond & Ben Arthur (local munros)

Abbey Cottage Tea Rooms

Attractive cottage tea rooms next to Sweetheart Abbey

☎ 01387 850377
✉ morag@
  abbeycottagetearoom.com
🌐 www.abbeycottagetearoom.
  com

Map ref 5 - NX97

26 Main Street, New Abbey,
DUMFRIES, Dumfries & Galloway,
DG2 8BY

☕ Open 10am-5pm (Apr-Oct) &
weekends (Nov, Dec, Mar); Tea served
all day daily; Closed Jan, Feb;
Booking possible; Seats 56 + 24
outside; No smoking

*Q*uality is the watchword at this highly acclaimed tea rooms, where morning coffee, light lunches and afternoon teas are all freshly prepared on the premises, using the best of ingredients from mainly local suppliers. Home-made pâtés, home-made organic bread and organic farmhouse cheeses are a speciality. On fine days additional seating is available in the garden, overlooking historic Sweetheart Abbey. There is a large public car park to the rear, and coach parties are welcome by prior arrangement.

Abbey Cottage also has its own well stocked gift shop, selling recipe books and oatcakes, preserves and pickles featured on the menu. No dogs.

The Tea Guild Award of Excellence 2004

RECOMMENDED IN THE AREA
Sweetheart Abbey; Dumfries Museum & Camera Obscura; Robert Burns Centre

*T*he Tea Room

A welcome oasis of calm in the middle of the busy Royal Mile

☎ 07771 501679
f 0131 538 4192
e info@the-tea-room.co.uk

Map ref 10 - NT27

158 Canongate, EDINBURGH, EH8 8DD

☕ Open 10.30am-4.30pm (please phone to check times in winter); Tea served all day; Closed Wed (winter); Booking possible (for groups); No Smoking

Discover what the future holds in store for you by having your tea leaves read here every Thursday between 2 and 5pm. This quirky practice is highly popular, and depends on real tea being prepared and served in proper teapots – something that goes without saying here. Set in Edinburgh's fashionable Royal Mile where much of the city's turbulent history took place, this quiet spot offers some respite from the hectic streets. Trish Noon and Joseph Winders have created a calm tea room with linen tablecloths and watercolours by local artists decorating the walls. The food itself is a complete distraction from what's going on around: all sorts of lunchtime dishes are listed on the menu, from soups to toasted sandwiches and filled baked potatoes, and delectable desserts. When it comes to tea time, you can choose a traditional afternoon version or a cream tea, with the scrumptious home-baked scones and interesting range of cakes to remind you of what afternoons are for.

RECOMMENDED IN THE AREA

Palace of Holyroodhouse; Edinburgh Castle; The People's Story

Kind Kyttock's Kitchen

Traditional Scottish tea rooms in a historic setting

📞 01337 857477

Map ref 10 - NO20

Cross Wynd, FALKLAND, Fife, KY15 7BE

☕ Open daily; Tea served 10.30am-5.30pm; Closed Mon 24 Dec-5 Jan; Booking possible Set tea price(s) £5.50; Seats 72; No Smoking No dogs

*T*he picturesque village of Falkland is dominated by Falkland Palace, the hunting palace of the Stuart monarchs, and close by is Kind Kyttock's tea rooms, where all the produce is made on the premises. A wide variety of snacks, soups, sandwiches, salads and sweets is served, and the set afternoon tea includes a pot of tea together with a scone and pancake, plus a choice of home-made preserves and two home-made cakes. Children are welcome and high chairs are provided. Free parking is available opposite the tea room, and you can book ahead for tea. A small selection of items is offered for sale. No dogs.

RECOMMENDED IN THE AREA
Falkland Palace; Lomond Hills; Loch Leven Castle

The Tea Guild Award of Excellence 2004.

The Old Course Hotel Golf Resort & Spa ★★★★★ ◉◖

Traditional afternoon tea, with a surprising variation

📞 01334 474371
📠 01334 477668
✉ reservations@
  oldcoursehotel.co.uk
🌐 www.oldcoursehotel.co.uk

Map ref 10 - NO51

ST ANDREWS, Fife, KY16 9SP
Close to A91 on outskirts of the city.
☕ Open daily; Tea served 2.30pm-4.30pm; Closed 25, 26 Dec; Booking advisable; Set tea price(s) £13.50, £20.00, £17.50, £24.00; Seats 50; No smoking areas; Parking 150 🛏 134 Rooms; S £230-£530, D £225-£545

*W*hether you are a golfer or not, sitting beside the most famous hole in the world of golf is sure to be a thrill. For those really not interested, the sea views will compensate, especially when accompanied by afternoon tea. In this traditional, even hallowed, setting, the last thing you might expect to find would be a newcomer calling itself the Chocolate Afternoon Tea. But here it is: chocolate scones, cakes, brownies,

gateaux, éclairs and tartlets can all be relished along with strawberries and chocolate sauce, and even a choice of five chocolate-based cocktails. Traditionalists need not despair for the cream tea is here too.

RECOMMENDED IN THE AREA
British Golf Museum; Cathedral; Castle & Visitor Centre

*M*iss Cranston's Tearooms

Stylish and exciting – a designer tea shop

☎ 0141 204 1122
📠 0141 620 0035
✉ claire@bradfordsltd.com
🌐 www.bradfordsbakers.com

Map ref 9 - NS66

33 Gordon Street, GLASGOW, G1 3PF
*Between Central Station and Buchanan
Street.*
☕ Open daily; Tea served 8am-5pm Mon-
Sat; Closed Sundays, 25 & 26 Dec, 1 & 2 Jan;
Booking possible; Set tea prices(s) £6.95;
Seats 110; No Smoking; Air con;
Guide dogs only

*K*ate Cranston owned several successful tea
rooms in Glasgow at the end of the 19th
century, so the use of her name here is highly
appropriate. The city's newest tea room is an
elegant space decorated with tall copper panels
etched with recipes, creating a restful and soothing
environment. It is already renowned for its afternoon
teas, when several varieties of loose leaf tea are
brewed to perfection and served with luxury
sandwiches, scones and pancakes with cream and
jam, and fancy cream cakes. Downstairs a bakery
and patisserie allows you to buy your favourite treats
and eat them at home.

RECOMMENDED IN THE AREA
*Glasgow Botanic Gardens; Tenement House;
The Tall Ship at Glasgow Harbour*

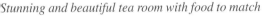

*W*illow Tea Rooms

Stunning and beautiful tea room with food to match

☎ 0141 204 5242
✉ buchananstreet@
willowtearooms.co.uk
🌐 www.willowtearooms.co.uk

Map ref 9 - NS66

97 Buchanan Street, GLASGOW,
G1 3HF
*In city centre, 5 mins' walk from Queen
St & Central train stations, 3 mins' walk
from Buchanan St tube station.*
☕ Open daily; Tea served 9am-
4.30pm Mon-Sat, 11am-4.15pm Sun
25, 26 Dec, 1, 2 Jan; Booking
possible; Set tea price(s) Afternoon
tea £8.95, cream tea before 12pm
£2.95; Seats 88; Air con; Guide dogs
only

*T*he Willow theme of placing strikingly beautiful furniture
against a calm and tasteful background works as well
here as at the sister tea shop in Sauchiehall Street. The
same architect, Charles Rennie Mackintosh, was
responsible for the designs at the turn of the last century,
when he created a series of teashops for Kate Cranston.
Upstairs is the blue Chinese Room with small furniture, while
downstairs the amazing high-backed chairs are impossible
to ignore. Tea is something of a distraction, though, with its
classic afternoon selection served with a
good range of fine teas. There are plenty of
savoury and sweet choices throughout the
day too.

RECOMMENDED IN THE AREA
*House for an Art Lover; The Lighthouse;
Clydebuilt*

161

WALK

Glasgow's Architecture

From the heart of the Merchant City to where it all started in the Old Town

From the tourist office in George Square turn left into Queen Street and cross the road to the Gallery of Modern Art. This was built as the residence of William Cunninghame, a tobacco lord, in 1778 and is the finest of these mansions in the city. Cross to Ingram Street continuing along past the imposing façade of the Corinthian. Turn right into Virginia Place and continue

WHAT TO LOOK FOR

Just north of the Cathedral Precinct is a pedestrian bridge that goes across the busy road to reach a large red sandstone school. This is the Martyrs' Public School, a traditional Glasgow public school but with one important difference. This one was designed by Charles Rennie Mackintosh.

through to Virginia Street. Like the rest of the Merchant City, the buildings here were built from the profits from the tobacco and sugar trade. At No 51 is Virginia Court where the tobacco merchants were based from 1817.

From Virginia Street turn left into Trongate, left into Hutcheson Street then left again, back into Ingram Street. The white square building with the spire opposite here is Hutchesons' Hall built in 1805 on the site of a previous hospice built by George and Thomas Hutcheson.

Continue along Ingram Street to St David's parish church, more often referred to as the Ramshorn Church because of the legend of St Mungo turning a stolen ram's head into stone on this spot. It is now a theatre facility for Strathclyde University. Continue along Ingram Street then, at the junction, turn left into High Street and proceed uphill. Pass Cathedral Square Gardens on the right, with an equestrian statue of William III, dressed as a Roman emperor. Across the High Street from here is Glasgow's oldest house, Provand's Lordship. Built around 1471 for the priest in charge of the St Nicholas

Hospital, it later became the house of the Canon of Barlanark, who was rector of the Lordship of Provan. Throughout its long history the house has had many uses but somehow survived development to become a museum. Opposite is Glasgow Cathedral; a fine example of medieval Scottish architecture, it is the only mainland cathedral to have emerged intact from the Reformation.

From Provand's Lordship turn left into Cathedral Street. Turn left again at the junction with Montrose Street and then right into George Street and back to George Square. Finish the walk by having a look at the rich ornamentation of the City Chambers, which dominates one end of the square. Built by the Victorian city fathers as a symbol of Glasgow's wealth and prosperity, it is still the municipal headquarters. Its exotic marble interior often moonlights as a film location.

DISTANCE: 2.5 miles (4km) 3hrs
START/FINISH: George Square (Tourist Office)
MAP: AA Street by Street Glasgow
TERRAIN : City streets
GRADIENT: Mostly level

*T*he Willow Tearoom

Stylish modern tea rooms in the city's heart

☎ 0141 3320521
✉ sauchiehallstreet@
willowtearooms.co.uk
ⓦ www.willowtearooms.co.uk

Map ref 9 - NS66

217 Sauchiehall Street, GLASGOW, G2 3EX
In city centre, 10 mins' walk from Queen St &
Charing Cross train stations, 5 mins' walk
from Cowcaddens tube station.
☕ Open daily; Tea served 9am-4.30pm
Mon-Sat, 11am-4.15pm Sun 25, 26 Dec, 1, 2
Jan; Booking possible; Set tea price(s)
Afternoon tea £8.95, cream tea before 12pm
£2.95; Seats 89; Smoking allowed in certain
areas; Air con; Guide dogs only

Stunning modern designs including tall silver chairs in futuristic styles and mirrored friezes are a talking point when guests first enter these smart tearooms. Located above a jewellery shop in this famous street, The Willow goes back to 1903 when Charles Rennie Mackintosh created a series of teashops for owner Kate Cranston. The food served here is more than a match for the striking settings, and afternoon tea is a popular ritual with the city's many tourists. Enjoy a selection of sandwiches, scones with preserves and cream, a choice of cakes and a delicious pot of loose leaf tea or a decent coffee.

The Tea Guild Award of Excellence 2004.

RECOMMENDED IN THE AREA
Pollock House; Glasgow Science Centre: Glasgow School of Art

---

*I*nverlochy Castle Hotel ★★★★ ◎◎◎

Imposing castle set against Ben Nevis amid glorious Scottish scenery

☎ 01397 702177
🖷 01397 702953
✉ info@inverlochy.co.uk
ⓦ www.
inverlochycastlehotel.com

Map ref 12 - NN17

Torlundy, FORT WILLIAM, Highland,
PH33 6SN
Accessible from either A82 Glasgow-
Fort William or A9 Edinburgh-
Dalwhinnie. Hotel 3m N of Fort William
on A82, in Torlundy.
☕ Open daily; Tea served 2pm-5pm;
Closed 6 Jan-12 Feb; Booking
essential; Set tea price(s) £20; Seats
30; Parking 17
🛏 17 Rooms; S £205-£290,
D £290-£395

In a splendidly romantic location, just three miles from Fort William, this grand castle stands overlooking its own loch, towards the valley of Lochy, in the foothills of Ben Nevis. Inverlochy is surrounded by extensive grounds, including a walled garden and tennis court, and was built by the first Lord Abinger in 1863. Queen Victoria visited in September 1873 and was very impressed. The interiors are lavishly appointed in the country house style, and tea is served in the Great Hall, the Drawing Room, or outside in fine weather. Full afternoon tea includes sandwiches, a selection of biscuits, scones and Dundee cake. No children, no dogs.

RECOMMENDED IN THE AREA
Glen Nevis; Nevis Range; Loch Ness

*I*nver Lodge Hotel ★★★ ✿

Modern hotel set amid a wild and wonderful landscape with thrilling views from its hilltop site

☎ 01571 844496   📠 01571 844395
✉ stay@inverlodge.com   🌐 www.inverlodge.com

Map ref 12 - NC02

LOCHINVER, Highland, IV27 4LU
A835 to Lochinver, continue through village and turn left after village hall, follow private rd for 0.5m.
🍽 Open daily; Tea served 2pm-5pm; Closed Nov-Mar; Booking possible; Seats 40; Parking 30
🛏 20 Rooms, D £140

RECOMMENDED IN THE AREA
Highland Stoneware; Ardvreck Castle; Culag Woods Nature Trail

*L*overs of the natural world will delight in the location of Inver Lodge, set high on a hill overlooking the fishing village of Lochinver and across the Minch towards the Western Isles. This is the ideal place to get away from it all. The two-hour drive from Inverness will take you through some stunning Highland scenery, and you might expect to see red and roe deer grazing in the grounds and perhaps a golden eagle soaring above. Abundant local produce is used to good effect across the menus at Inver Lodge, and at tea you can sample Highland smoked salmon sandwiches, or roast beef with horseradish among the selection. The set meal comprises a home-baked scone with raspberry or strawberry conserve and clotted cream, fruitcake, shortbread and a pot of tea or coffee. Tea is served in the spacious upstairs lounge and bar, which takes full advantage of the views and where, in winter, a log fire burns in the Scots Pine fireplace. No dogs.

*P*ool House ★ ★ ★ ◉◉

Romantic retreat on the shore of Loch Ewe

☏ 01445 781272
🖷 01445 781403
✉ enquiries@
poolhousehotel.com
🌐 www.poolhousehotel.com

Map ref 11 - NG88

POOLEWE, Highland, IV22 2LD
*6m N of Gairloch on the A832.
Located in the middle of Poolewe
village, next to the bridge at the edge
of the sea.*
☕ Open daily; Tea served 2.30pm-
6pm; Booking essential in winter;
Set tea price(s) £9.95-£14.00; Seats
14; No smoking; Children not
admitted; Parking 20
🛏 5 Rooms; S £80-£95, D £240-£330

*D*ating back over 300 years, this historic house is set between loch and mountain amid majestic Highland scenery. The hotel is filled with antiques, paintings and objects of interest, and was once the home of Osgood Mackenzie, founder of Inverewe Garden – now owned by National Trust Scotland. The Victorian-style Library Drawing Room is the setting for tea, where the tables are graced with lace cloths and Coalport china, and finger sandwiches, cakes, tarts and cream scones are served. Reservations are recommended to avoid disappointment and are obligatory in winter. The drawing room overlooks the sea, and binoculars are provided for watching the seals, otters and birds.

RECOMMENDED IN THE AREA
*Inverewe Garden; Marine Cruises from Gairloch;
Beinn Eighe Nature Reserve*

*W*estin Turnberry Resort ★ ★ ★ ★ ★ ◉

Elaborate afternoon teas to take the mind off golf

☏ 01655 331000
🖷 01655 331706
✉ turnberry@westin.com
🌐 www.westin.com/turnberry

Map ref 9 - NS02

TURNBERRY, KA26 9LT
*From Glasgow take the A77/M77 S
towards Stranraer, 2m past
Kirkoswald, follow signs for A719
Turnberry Village, hotel 500mtrs
on right.*
☕ Open daily; Tea served 12.30pm-
5pm daily; Booking possible; Set tea
price(s) £17.50, £22.50; Seats 60;
Parking 200
🛏 221 Rooms; S £115-£715,
D £149-£770

*T*his world-famous golfing resort hotel knows a thing or two about entertaining. From its magnificent location overlooking the Atlantic coastline, with 800 acres of beautiful grounds surrounding it, it offers the perfect retreat or leisure break. Golf is at its heart, and champions past, present and future have played the game here, and brought a wide following in their wake. One of the greatest pleasures of a visit, golfing or otherwise, is the afternoon tea served in the Ailsa lounge. French pastries, pancakes and crumpets, and scones with clotted cream are all part of the package, with a choice of fine teas to accompany them.

RECOMMENDED IN THE AREA
*Loudoun Castle Theme Park;
Burns National Heritage Park;
David Livingstone Centre*

WALK

Telford's Caledonian Canal

Of all the canals built during this era the Caledonian Canal, designed by Thomas Telford and completed in 1847, is undoubtedly the most impressive. Its 60-mile (97km) length includes an impressive flight of eight locks known as Neptune's Staircase.

From the car park, cross the main road (A830) and go through a metal gate on to the canal towpath. On your left is Neptune's Staircase, a flight of eight locks that raises the canal 64ft (19m) in height. Above the locks, yachts lie moored in a sheltered basin.

Follow the towpath, with the canal on your left, for approximately 2.5 miles (4km). The ground drops steeply to the right and through gaps in the woodland there are fine views of the Ben Nevis range and of Inverlochy Castle Hotel, a Gothic mansion that is now one of Scotland's most exclusive hotels.

The canal and towpath bridge a stream, with some houses visible below. Continue for 20yds (18m), then turn right down a path between the trees. Beyond the gate at the bottom, turn sharp right to follow the stream through the tunnel under the canal and past a weir. Reaching an intersection, turn sharp right to return to the canal and right again along the towpath.

On the return walk there are fine views along Loch Linnhe to the Corran Narrows and of the 4,406ft (1,343m) summit of Ben Nevis, Britain's highest mountain. The town of Fort William, on the east shore of the loch, was still a military garrison at the time of the canal's construction.

Pass Neptune's Store, a small post office and shop, offering tourist information, toilets and facilities for yachtsmen (limited winter opening). The bow-windowed cottages overlooking Neptune's Staircase date from the early 1800s. Cross the canal by the lock gates to return to the car park.

WHAT TO LOOK FOR

The old capstans beside the locks had to be rotated with long poles to operate the gates. This was heavy work, since 126 full turns were required to ascend the staircase. It was not until the 1960s that the system was converted to hydraulic power. Also worth noting are the two Inverlochy Castles located across the Lochy and, upstream, the remains of two Tor Castles.

DISTANCE: 5 miles (8km)
START/FINISH: Banavie Station car park
MAP: OS Outdoor Leisure 38
TERRAIN: Waterside and woodland
GRADIENT: Level, apart from one short descent

Scottish Hotels

These hotels also offer afternoon tea. Remember you may have to book, so please telephone in advance to avoid disappointment.

ABERDEEN CITY

★★★ Aberdeen
  Marriott Hotel
Overton Circle Dyce AB21 7AZ
☎ 01224 770011 🖷 01224 722347
e: reservations.aberdeen@
marriotthotels.co.uk

★★★ Ardoe House
South Deeside Road Blairs
AB12 5YP
☎ 01224 860600 🖷 01224 861283
e: ardoe@macdonald-hotels.co.uk

★★★★ The Marcliffe at
  Pitfodels
North Deeside Road AB15 9YA
☎ 01224 861000 🖷 01224 868860
e: enquiries@marcliffe.com

ABERDEENSHIRE

★★ Balgonie Country
  House Hotel
Braemar Place Ballater AB35 5NQ
☎ 013397 55482 🖷 013397 55482
e: balgoniech@aol.com

★★ Darroch Learg Hotel
Braemar Road Balleter AB35 5UX
☎ 013397 55443 🖷 013397 55252
e: nigel@darrochlearg.co.uk

★★★ Thainstone House
Inverurie AB51 5NT
☎ 01467 621643 🖷 01467 625084
e: thainstone@
macdonald-hotels.co.uk

★★★ Waterside Inn
Fraserburgh Road Peterhead
AB42 3BN
☎ 01779 471121 🖷 01779 470670
e: waterside@
macdonald-hotels.co.uk

ANGUS

★★★ Castleton
  House Hotel
Castleton of Eassie Glamis
DD8 1SJ
☎ 01307 840340 🖷 01307 840506
e: hotel@castletonglamis.co.uk

CITY OF EDINBURGH

★★★ Carlton Hotel
North Bridge Edinburgh EH1 1SD
☎ 0131 472 3000 🖷 0131 556 2691
e: carlton@
paramount-hotels.co.uk

★★★ George
  Inter-Continental
19-21 George Street Edinburgh
EH2 2PB
☎ 0131 225 1251 🖷 0131 226 5644
e: edinburgh@interconti.com

★★★ Menzies
  Belford Hotel
69 Belford Road
Edinburgh EH4 3DG
☎ 0131 332 2545 🖷 0131 332 3805
e: belford@menzies-hotels.co.uk

★★★ Edinburgh
  Marriott Hotel
111 Glasgow Road
Edinburgh EH12 8NF
☎ 0131 334 9191 🖷 0131 316 4507
e:edinburgh@marriotthotels.co.uk

★★★ Norton House
  Hotel & Restaurant
Ingliston Edinburgh EH28 8LX
☎ 0131 333 1275 🖷 0131 333 5305
e: nortonhouse-cro@
handpicked.co.uk

★★★ Marriott
  Dalmahoy Hotel
  & Country Club
Kirknewton Edinburgh EH27 8EB
☎ 0131 333 1845 🖷 0131 333 1433

★★★ The Bonham
  Hotel
35 Drumsheugh Gardens
Edinburgh EH3 7RN
☎ 0131 623 6060 🖷 0131 226 6080
e: reserve@thebonham.com

★★★★★ The Balmoral
  Hotel
1 Princes Street
Edinburgh EH2 2EQ
☎ 0131 556 2414 🖷 0131 557 8740
e: reservations@
thebalmoralhotel.com

★★★★★ The Sheraton
  Grand Hotel & Spa
1 Festival Square
Edinburgh EH3 9SR
☎ 0131 229 9131 🖷 0131 228 4510
e: grandedinburgh.
sheraton@sheraton.com

★★★★★ The Scotsman
20 North Bridge
Edinburgh EH1 1YT
☎ 0131 556 5565 🖷 0131 652 3652
e: reservations@
thescotsmanhotelgroup.co.uk

CITY OF GLASGOW

★★★ One Devonshire
  Gardens
1 Devonshire Gardens
Glasgow G12 0UX
☎ 0141 339 2001 🖷 0141 337 1663
e: reservations@
onedevonshiregardens.com

★★★ Millennium Hotel
  Glasgow
George Square Glasgow G2 1DS
☎ 0141 332 6711 🖷 0141 332 4264
e: reservations.glasgow@
mill-cop.com

★★★ Langs Hotel
2 Port Dundas Place
Glasgow G2 3LD
☎ 0141 333 1500 🖷 0141 333 5700
e: genman@langshotel.fsnet.co.uk

★★★ Milton Hotel &
  Leisure Club
27 Washington Street
Glasgow G3 8AZ
☎ 0141 222 2929 🖷 0141 222 2626
e: sales@miltonhotels.com

DUMFRIES & GALLOWAY

★★★★ **Cally Palace Hotel**
Gatehouse of Fleet DG7 2DL
☎ 01557 814341 🖷 01557 814522
e: info@callypalace.co.uk

★ **Well View Hotel**
Ballplay Road Moffat
DG10 9JU
☎ 01683 220184 🖷 01683 220088
e: info@wellview.co.uk

★★★★ **North West Castle Hotel**
Stranraer DG9 8EH
☎ 01776 704413 🖷 01776 702646
e: info@northwestcastle.co.uk

FIFE

★★★★ **Balbirnie House**
Balbirnie Park Markinch KY7 6NE
☎ 01592 610066 🖷 01592 610529
e: info@balbirnie.co.uk

★★★ **Rufflets Country House & Garden Restaurant**
Strathkinness Low Road
St Andrews KY16 9TX
☎ 01334 472594 🖷 01334 478703
e: reservations@rufflets.co.uk

★★★ **St Andrews Golf Hotel**
40 The Scores
St Andrews KY16 9AS
☎ 01334 472611 🖷 01334 472188
e: reception@standrews-golf.co.uk

★★★★ **Rusacks Hotel**
Pilmour Links
St Andrews KY16 9JQ
☎ 0870 400 8128 🖷 01334 477896
e: rusacks@
macdonald-hotels.co.uk

HIGHLAND

★★★★ **Culloden House Hotel**
Culloden Inverness IV2 7BZ
☎ 01463 790461 🖷 01463 792181
e: reserv@cullodenhouse.co.uk

★★★★ **Inverness Marriott Hotel**
Culcabock Road Inverness IV2 3LP
☎ 01463 237166 🖷 01463 225208
e: events@marriotthotels.co.uk

★★★★ **Golf View Hotel & Leisure Club**
The Seafront Nairn IV12 4HD
☎ 01667 452301 🖷 01667 455267
e: golfview@morton-hotels.com

★★★ **Loch Torridon Country House Hotel**
Torridon IV22 2EY
☎ 01445 791242 🖷 01445 791296
e: stay@lochtorridonhotel.com

PERTH & KINROSS

★★★★★ **The Gleneagles Hotel**
Auchterarder PH3 1NF
☎ 01764 662231 🖷 01764 662134
e: resort.sales@gleneagles.com

★★★ **Kinnaird**
Kinnaird Estate Dunkeld PH8 0LB
☎ 01796 482440 🖷 01796 482289
e: enquiry@kinnairdestate.com

★★★ **Ballathie House Hotel**
Stanley Kinclaven PH1 4QN
☎ 01250 883268 🖷 01250 883396
e: email@ballathiehousehotel.com

★★★ **Kinfauns Castle**
Kinfauns Perth PH2 7JZ
☎ 01738 620777 🖷 01738 620778
e: email@kinfaunscastle.co.uk

SOUTH AYRSHIRE

★★★★ **Fairfield House Hotel**
12 Fairfield Road Ayr KA7 2AR
☎ 01292 267461 🖷 01292 261456
e: reservations@
fairfieldhotel.co.uk

★★★ **Lochgreen House**
Monktonhill Road Southwood
Troon KA10 7EN
☎ 01292 313343 🖷 01292 318661
e: lochgreen@costley-hotels.co.uk

★★★★ **Marine Hotel**
Crosbie Road TROON KA10 6HE
☎ 01292 314444 🖷 01292 316922
e: marine@paramount-hotels.co.uk

SOUTH LANARKSHIRE

★★★★ **Crutherland Country House Hotel**
Strathaven Road
East Kilbride G75 0QZ
☎ 01355 577000 🖷 01355 220855
e: crutherland@
macdonald-hotels.co.uk

STIRLING

★★★★ **Forest Hills Hotel**
Kinlochard Aberfoyle FK8 3TL
☎ 01877 387277 🖷 01877 387307
e: forest_hills@
macdonald-hotels.co.uk

★★★ **Roman Camp Country House Hotel**
Callander FK17 8BG
☎ 01877 330003 🖷 01877 331533
e: mail@roman-camp-hotel.co.uk

★★★ **Cromlix House Hotel**
Kinbuck Nr Dunblane FK15 9JT
☎ 01786 822125 🖷 01786 825450

e: reservations@cromlixhouse.com

WEST DUNBARTONSHIRE

★★★★★ **De Vere Cameron House**
Balloch G83 8QZ
☎ 01389 755565 🖷 01389 759522
e: reservations@
cameronhouse.co.uk

★★★★ **Beardmore Hotel**
Beardmore Street
CLYDEBANK G81 4SA
☎ 0141 951 6000 🖷 0141 951 6018
e: beardmore.hotel@hci.co.uk

WEST LOTHIAN

★★★★ **Houstoun House**
Uphall EH52 6JS
☎ 01506 853831 🖷 01506 854220
e: houstoun@macdonald-
hotels.co.uk

Wales

Chief among teatime savouries in Wales must be the ever-popular Welsh rarebit: hot toast topped with a thickened sauce made from sharp cheese and local ale. Laverbread, edible seaweed, is another Welsh speciality, which can be cooked in butter and lemon juice and served on toast. Laverbread mixed with oatmeal is fried into little cakes, which are sometimes eaten at breakfast. In coastal areas you will also encounter cockles and mussels as a local delicacy.

Cawl cennin, leek soup, is a great favourite, the leek being the Welsh national emblem. Leeks also combine well with the creamy local cheeses to make a tasty savoury tart. Caerphilly cheese, known locally as 'the crumblies', is mild and tangy and was traditionally favoured by miners for their lunch boxes.

Among the tea breads are bara brith, a yeasted fruit bread, baked as a loaf and served sliced with butter – available in all good tea shops – and Welsh cakes, a kind of scone, mixed quite stiff in this case to achieve a firm consistency, and fried on a griddle or frying pan. Welsh curd cakes are pastry tartlets filled with a mixture of junket, cake crumbs, butter, sugar and a few currants. Snowden pudding is a steamed suet pudding capped with raisins, which for special occasions might be accompanied by a wine sauce.

*G*walia Tea Rooms

Authentic tea room serving Welsh speciality foods

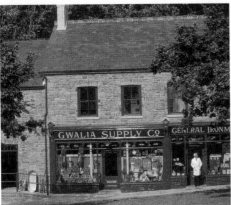

☎ 01222 566985
🖷 01222 586985

Map ref 2 - ST17

The Museum of Welsh Life,
ST FAGANS, Cardiff, CF5 6XB
🍴 Open daily; Tea served 10am-
4.45pm; Closed 24, 25 Dec, 1 Jan;
Booking possible; Set tea price(s)
£5.00; Visa & Mastercard accepted;
Seats 36; No Smoking

A fascinating museum of Welsh life through the ages is the setting for this atmospheric tea room decorated and furnished in authentic 1920s style. Many of the buildings which form part of the museum have been moved stone by stone from all over Wales, and one such is the old general store which houses the Gwalia. Bentwood chairs, an etched glass screen and old photographs set the scene for the traditional tea menu, with its home-made cakes, and local specialities like Welsh rarebit, Teisen Lap (light and spicy fruit cake), Gwalia rock cake, and an excellent selection of speciality teas.

The Tea Guild Award of Excellence 2004

RECOMMENDED IN THE AREA
*Museum of Welsh Life; Cardiff Castle;
Llandaff Cathedral*

WALK

The Tracks of Industry

A walk following the course of a disused railway line in the county of Cardiff through the former industrial heartland of Wales

he Taff Trail runs, in its ntirety, from Brecon to ardiff; this section of the ail leads along part of the rmer Barry and Rhymney ilway lines, skirting the illside above the River Taff, e original means of loving cargoes from the hondda Valley mines to e southern shipping ports, ld from there to all over e world.

tart at the Treforest Park nd Ride, at the railway ation, and near the niversity of Glamorgan, riginally founded as the outh Wales and

Monmouthshire School of Mines. To reach the old railway bed, cross the footbridge and go down the slope. Cross into Castle Street; at the end of the street, cross Forest Road and the pedestrian bridge over the Taff. Bear left to go under the road bridge and follow the pavement under the motorway bridge. Cross the road with care. Go round to the left and into Cemetery Road.

Turn right and pass the cemetery and crematorium. Cremation was made legal in 1884, after local man Dr William Price had been prosecuted for cremating his baby son Iesu. Follow the Taff Trail sign to the right. The track passes between the houses of *Ryhdy felin*, whose name probably derives from *rhyd felen*, 'yellow ford': iron in the clay turned the water here a distinct yellow.

Presently the trail moves into oak woodland and

passes the remains of an old colliery on the hill to the left. Above the trees, glimpses of sheep grazing on the mountain recall the pre-steam, pre-industrial era, when travellers admired the natural drama of the 'Glamorgan Alps'. At Nantgarw the trail twists down into another estate and across the road on the valley floor, before climbing to the top of the opposite ridge.

As the trail approaches the beech woods of Fforest Fawr, it passes T^y Rhiw Farm, built before the railways and the coal boom. You can leave the trail here, following the sign left past the farm, to descend to Taff's Well station for the train back to Treforest. But it is worth continuing to Castell Coch, the fairytale 'red castle' designed by William Burges. It's 1.25 miles (2.4km) on foot or by bus from Tongwynlais to Taff's Well station.

DISTANCE: 6 miles (9.6km) to Taff's Well; 1 mile (1.6km) to Castell Coch
START/FINISH: Treforest Park & Ride (return by train from Taff's Well station).
MAP: OS Explorer 151
TERRAIN : Streets, paths, tracks - can be muddy
GRADIENT: Level, with one steep stretch

*B*adgers Café

Llandudno's legendary tea room and patisserie located among the town centre shops

☎ 01492 871649
✉ manager@badgersgroup.co.uk
🌐 www.badgersgroup.co.uk

Map ref 5 - SH78

The Victoria Shopping Mall, Mostyn Street, LLANDUDNO, Conwy, LL30 2NG

☕ Open 9.30am-5pm; Tea served all day; Closed 25-26 Dec, 1Jan, Easter Sun; Set tea price(s) £4.60, £6.25, £10.95; Seats 70; No Smoking; Air con

Conveniently located in the main shopping area of Llandudno, with a multi-storey car park close at hand, Badgers is the perfect place to rest, refuel and recuperate during a serious shopping expedition. The town's Victorian traditions are upheld, with waitresses – known as Badgers' nippies – dressed in period costume. Regional specialities include Welsh rarebit, Welsh cakes, Welsh cheese salads, and bara brith, and home-roasted meats are featured among the sandwich fillings. There are three set teas: Welsh Cream Tea with scones, jam and cream and bara brith; Garden Tea with a sandwich and bara brith; and – the ultimate treat – Victorian Tea with a sandwich, bara brith, scones with jam and cream, and cake. All the cakes at Badgers are home made in the bakery upstairs, including patisserie items such as swan meringues, dragon eclairs and ice mice. A cake boxing service is also available. A harpist occasionally entertains the customers.

The Tea Guild Award of Excellence 2004.

RECOMMENDED IN THE AREA
Bodnant Gardens; Snowdonia National Park; Victorian Tramway to Summit of Great Orme

Osborne House ★★★★

Beautifully renovated Victorian town house in a popular resort setting

☎ 01492 860330
📠 01492 860791
✉ sales@osbornehouse.com
🌐 www.osbornehouse.com

Map ref 5 - SH78

17 North House, LLANDUDNO,
Conwy, LL30 2LP
Exit A55 expressway at junct 19.
Follow signs for Llandudno then
Promenade. Continue until junction,
turn right. Osborne House on left
opposite pier entrance.
🍵 Open Tue-Sat; Tea served 2pm-
6pm; Closed Sun, Mon, Christmas
week; No smoking areas; Air con
🛏 6 Rooms; S £130-£200,
D £130-£200

Lovingly transformed over a number of years, this impressive all-suite hotel has retained much of its period character. The marbled entrance hall, Victorian fireplaces, ornate ceilings and sparkling chandeliers provide the backdrop for some fine antique pieces and original artwork. Afternoon tea is served in the lounge area or café, and there are a couple of tables outside for fine weather. Options at tea-time are the traditional version with a cucumber sandwich, scone, jam and cream, or the Champagne Tea comprising smoked salmon sandwich, scone, jam and cream with half a bottle of champagne for two people. Light bites and main meals are also available. Older children welcome. No dogs.

RECOMMENDED IN THE AREA

Snowdonia; Portmeirion Italianate Village; Conwy Castle

173

St Tudno Hotel ★★ ◉◉◉

Beautiful hotel with fine sea views enjoyed from comfortable lounges, renowned
for its award-winning teas

☎ 01492 874411
📠 01492 860407
📧 sttudnohotel@btinternet.com
🌐 www.st-tudno.co.uk

Map ref 5 - SH78

The Promenade, LLANDUDNO, Conwy,
LL30 2LP
On reaching Promenade drive towards the
pier, hotel opposite pier entrance & lawns.
🍵 Open daily; Tea served 2.30pm-5.30pm
daily; Set tea price(s) £10.95; Seats 40; No
smoking areas; Parking 11
🛏 19 Rooms; S £70-£80, D £88-£200

*A*fternoon tea doesn't come much better than this – and that's official. The award-winning teas served at this lovely hotel could be judged as excellent by the extent of the afternoon tea menu, where visitors can browse through pages of tempting choices. But the proof of the pudding is in the eating, and the St Tudno's afternoon choices are truly delicious. The Traditional Welsh tea and the De Luxe selection come with a pot of loose-leaf speciality tea from around 14 classic choices: from India there's Assam and Darjeeling, from Sri Lanka you'll find Uva and Ceylon, and the four representatives of China are Formosa, Lapsang Souchong, Gunpowder, and Keemun. There are separate lists of sandwiches, savouries, home-made cakes and strawberries and cream for the perfect DIY tea. The family-run team led by Janette and Martin Bland is friendly, natural and welcoming, and the lounge with its glorious sea views is most inviting.

RECOMMENDED IN THE AREA
Great Orme Headland; Conwy Castle; Bodnant
Gardens

*C*emlyn Restaurant and Teashop

Centrally located in Harlech's High Street – a tea shop by day and a restaurant by night

☎ 01766 780425
✉ geoffrey-cole@talkgas.net
🌐 www.cemlynrestaurant.co.uk

Map ref 5 - SH53

High Street, HARLECH, Gwynedd, LL46 2YA
On the High Street, next to the Post Office.
🍵 Open 11am-4pm; Tea served all day; closed Mon (ex BHs), Jan, Feb, Mar; Booking possible; Set tea price(s) £12; Seats 30; No Smoking; No children under 7 please; Credit Cards only accepted for sales over £10

A tea shop and restaurant with rooms, Cemlyn is happily situated to provide views of Harlech's 13th-century castle, Royal St David's Golf Course, the mountains and the sea. Both cigarettes and tea bags are banned from this no-smoking, all-tea leaf establishment, which makes an uncompromising commitment to quality. An eclectic choice of teas, tisanes and infusions is offered alongside home-made brownies, tea cakes, scones and regional favourites such as Welsh cakes and bara brith. Light lunches are served and even the sandwiches are made on home-made bread. A patio area is provided for outdoor seating in fine weather, and bed and breakfast accommodation is available for guests wishing to sleep over. Tea, coffee, preserves, recipes and guide books are sold on the premises for customers to enjoy at home. Children over seven are welcome, and dogs are permitted outside on the patio.

Runner up in The Tea Guild's 'Top Tea Place 2004' Awards.

RECOMMENDED IN THE AREA
Snowdonia National Park; Harlech Castle; West Coast of Wales

*L*langoed Hall ★★★★ ❀ ❀

Creeper-clad Jacobean/Edwardian great house, where important events such as afternoon tea are cherished

☎ 01874 754525
🖷 01874 754545
✉
llangoed_hall_co_wales_uk@
compuserve.com
🌐 www.llangoedhall.com

Map ref 2 - SO41

LLYSWEN, Powys, LD3 0YP
A470 through village for 2m. Hotel drive on right.
☕ Open daily; Tea served 2pm-5pm; Set tea price(s) £7.50, £8.00, £14.50; Seats 20; Parking 80
🛏 23 Rooms; S £120-£160, D £220-£260

*T*he Welsh Parliament once stood on this spot, and the great country house that is now Llangoed Hall is suitably impressive. Formerly known as a castle, it is a clever combination of the original Jacobean mansion and the best of Edwardian styles. It stands in a beautiful lush valley, with stunning views across the Wye Valley to the Black Mountains beyond. Walled gardens and spacious parkland complete the idyllic picture. Indoors there are plenty of striking features, like the 95-foot long pillared gallery, carved timber staircase, and panelled library. Another notable highlight is the serving of afternoon tea in the gracious lounge, the bright garden room, the cheerful morning room, and the grand library itself. Turn up any afternoon for the cream tea, and enjoy scones, clotted cream, jam and Welsh cakes. Twenty-four hours' notice is required for the speciality full afternoon tea, but it is well worth planning in advance. Children over 8 years of age are welcome in the tea toom.

The Tea Guild Award of Excellence 2004.

RECOMMENDED IN THE AREA
Hay on Wye book & antique shops, River Wye, Elan Valley & reservoirs

WALK

Powys - Felin Fach

Climb into a land of rolling hills and distant mountain views on the edge of the Brecon Beacons National Park

From the village centre, pass the Griffin Inn and turn left to the Plough and Harrow. Go straight on along the 'No through road' and cross a stile by a footpath sign. Head for some steps leading up the bank to the A470, cross over and descend to a footbridge. Cross the field, climbing the slope to a stile. Continue ahead through the next pasture, keeping the boundary hedge on your right. Descend to a stile, cross the lane to two galvanised gates and take the one on the right. Continue ahead along the field edge

and make your way to the top corner. At this point join a track running between trees and hedgerows and follow it to the road. Turn right and then swing left at the next junction, pass several cottages and on reaching the buildings of Old Pengoyfford, turn left through the gate into a field. Cross the field diagonally to a gate in the hedgerow and

head for two gates in the opposite boundary. Ascend the field slope to a gate by some trees and follow the track to a stile. Keep ahead through the trees and vegetation to reach a gate. Cross the pasture to a galvanised gate and then descend the field slope alongside a line of trees. Veer right to Hillis Farm and follow the track to the road. Turn left and make for the village of Llanfilo. Pass the church and when the road bends right, swing left to join a track. At the next junction turn left and follow the track until eventually it meets a lane. Turn right and pass a large house with a cattle-grid at the entrance. Turn right just beyond the house and follow the path across several fields to the A470. Retrace your steps to the village centre.

DISTANCE: 7 miles/11.3km
START/FINISH: Felin Fach
MAP: OS Explorer OL12 and OL13
TERRAIN: Field paths and tracks. Stretches of quiet roads
GRADIENT: Undulating landscape. No dramatic ascents

Welsh Hotels

These hotels also offer afternoon tea. Remember you may have to book, so please telephone in advance to avoid disappointment.

BRIDGEND

★ ★ ★ ★ Coed-Y-Mwstwr Hotel
Coychurch Bridgend CF35 6AF
☎ 01656 860621 📠 01656 863122
e: anything@coed-y-mwstwr.com

CARDIFF

★ ★ ★ ★ Cardiff Marriott Hotel
Mill Lane CF10 1EZ
☎ 029 2039 9944 📠 029 2039 5578
e: sara.nurse@
marriotthotels.co.uk

★ ★ ★ ★ Angel Hotel
Castle Street CF10 1SZ
☎ 029 2064 9200 📠 029 2039 6212
e: angelreservations@
paramount-hotels.co.uk

★ ★ ★ ★ ★ The St David's Hotel & Spa
Havannah Street CF10 5SD
☎ 029 2045 4045 029 2048 7056
e: reservations@
thestdavidshotel.com

★ ★ ★ ★ Copthorne Hotel Cardiff-Caerdydd
Copthorne Way Culverhouse Cross CF5 6DH
☎ 029 2059 9100 📠 029 2059 9080
e: sales.cardiff@mill-cop.com

★ ★ ★ ★ Hanover International Hotel & Club
Schooner Way Atlantic Wharf CF10 4RT
☎ 029 2047 5000 📠 029 2048 1491

CEREDIGION

★ ★ ★ Ynyshir Hall
Machynlleth
EglwysFach SY20 8TA
☎ 01654 781209 📠 01654 781366
e: info@ynyshir-hall.co.uk

CONWY

★ ★ ★ ★ Bodysgallen Hall
Llandudno LL30 1RS
☎ 01492 584466 📠 01492 582519
e: info@bodysgallen.com

FLINTSHIRE

★ ★ ★ ★ De Vere St David's Park
St Davids Park Ewloe
Nr Chester CH5 3YB
☎ 01244 520800 📠 01244 520930
e: reservations.stdavids@
devere-hotels.com

GWYNEDD

★ ★ Maes y Neuadd Country House Hotel
Talsarnau LL47 6YA
☎ 01766 780200 📠 01766 780211
e: maes@neuadd.com

★ ★ ★ Seiont Manor Hotel
Llanrug Caernnarfon LL55 2AQ
☎ 01286 673366 📠 01286 672840
e: seiontmanorcro@
handpicked.co.uk

★ ★ ★ Castell Deudraeth
Portmeirlon LL48 6EN
☎ 01766 772400 📠 01766 771771
e: castell@
portmeirion-village.com

NEWPORT

★ ★ ★ ★ ★ The Celtic Manor Resort
Coldra Woods Newport NP18 1HQ
☎ 01633 413000 📠 01633 412910
e: postbox@celtic-manor.com

POWYS

★ ★ ★ Lake Country House Hotel
Llangammarch Wells LD4 4BS
☎ 01591 620202 📠 01591 620457
e: info@lakecountryhouse.co.uk

RHONDDA CYNON TAFF

★ ★ ★ ★ Miskin Manor Hotel & Health Club
Groes Faen Pontyclun Miskin CF72 8ND
☎ 01443 224204 📠 01443 237606
e: info@miskin-manor.co.uk

SWANSEA

★ ★ ★ ★ Swansea Marriott Hotel
The Maritime Quarter SA1 3SS
☎ 01792 642020 📠 01792 650345

Index

182

Credits

Acknowledgments

The Automobile Association would like to thank THE TEA COUNCIL in providing the following images for this book.
1, 2t, 2b, 4, 5, 12, 13l, 13c, 13, 14, 15t, 15b, 17

The rest of the photographs in this book are held in the Association's own library (AA WORLD TRAVEL LIBRARY) with contributions from the following.

Adrian Baker 118, 135tl; Peter Baker 60br, 125tl; Stewart Bates 38; Jeff Beazley 113; M Birkitt 114t, 114b, 117; EA Bowness 54; Peter Brown 135br; Ian Burgum 171br; Michael Busselle 80, 133t, 133b; Derek Croucher 173; Steve Day 52, 69; Derek Forss 176br, 32, 65, 130, 139br; Stephen Gibson 157; Van Greaves 128; T Griffiths 84; Richard Ireland 127, 144; Caroline Jones 79, 122b, 170; J W Jorgenson 169t, 169b; Max Jourdan 106; Andrew Lawson 4, 37, 44, 58t, 58b, 125br; Simon McBride 104tl; Tom Mackie 49b, 112, 129; S & O Mathews 11br, 60tl, 82tl, 153; Colin Molyneux 177br; Robert Mort 12, 91br; Roger Moss 42b, 48, 122t; Rich Newton 146t; Neil Ray 42t; Graham Rowatt 41; Clive Sawyer 13l, 13r; Barrie Smith 104br; Tony Souter 11tl, 109, 113 Rick Strange 91tl, 139tl; Richard Surman 49t; David Tarn 146; Martin Trelawny 86b, 120tl; Andy Tryner 38, 39; Richard Turpin 97tl, 118t; Roy Victor 97br; Wyn Voysey 36, 67, 71, 72tl, 142; Ronnie Weir 166br; Jonathan Welsh 70; Stephen Whitehorne 162, 166tl; Linda Whitwam 151br; Harry Williams 78, 82br, 171tl; Peter Wilson 151tl; Tim Woodcock 177tl

Walks on pages 72, 76, 91, 97, 104, 111, 125, 120, 139, 135, 177 researched by Nick Channer.

Other walks by: 44 Des Hannigan; 52 Bill Birkett; 60 Sue Viccars; 82 Rebecca Ford; 151 David Winpenny; 166 Hamish Scott; 162 Hugh Taylor & Moira McCossan; 177 Nia Williams

Please send this form to:
    AA
    Lifestyle Guides,
    The Automobile Association,
    Fanum House,
    Basingstoke RG21 4EA

or fax: 01256 491647
or e-mail: lifestyleguides@theAA.com

Readers' Report form

If you've enjoyed Afternoon Tea at a teashop, tea room or in a hotel not recommended in this guide, why not tell us about it?

Please note, however, that if you have a complaint to make during a visit, we strongly recommend that you discuss the matter with the establishment management there and then so that they have a chance to put things right before your visit is spoilt. The AA does not undertake to arbitrate between you and the establishment, or to obtain compensation or engage in correspondence.

Date:

Your name (block capitals)

Your address (block capitals)

....

....

....

.... e-mail address:

Comments (please include the name & address of the establishment)

....

....

....

....

....

....

(please attach a separate sheet if necessary)

We may use information we hold about you to write, e-mail or telephone you about other products and services offered by us and our carefully selected partners. Information may be disclosed to other companies in the Centrica group (including those using the British Gas, Scottish Gas, One-Tel and AA brands) but we can assure you that we will not disclose it to third parties.

Please tick here if you DO NOT wish to receive details of other products or services from the AA. ☐

PTO

Have you bought any other AA Britain's Best guides or other accommodation, restaurant, pub, or food guides recently? If yes, which ones?

....

....

Why did you buy the guide? To find a place for tea..

For a celebration   On holiday   While shopping

Break while travelling

other...

How often do you visit a place for tea? (circle one choice)

more than once a month   once a month   once in 2-3 months

once in six months   once a year   less than once a year

Please answer these questions to help us make improvements to the guide:

Which of these factors are most important when choosing a place for tea?

Price   Location   Awards/ratings   Service

Decor/surroundings   Previous experience
Recommendation

Other (please state):..

Do you read the editorial features in the guide?.......................................

Do you use the location atlas?...

Which elements of the guide do you find the most useful when choosing somewhere to have tea?

Description   Photo   Rating

Can you suggest any improvements to the guide?

....

....

....

....

Please send this form to:
AA
Lifestyle Guides,
The Automobile Association,
Fanum House,
Basingstoke RG21 4EA

Readers' Report form

or fax: 01256 491647
or e-mail: lifestyleguides@theAA.com

If you've enjoyed Afternoon Tea at a teashop, tea room or in a hotel not recommended in this guide, why not tell us about it?

Please note, however, that if you have a complaint to make during a visit, we strongly recommend that you discuss the matter with the establishment management there and then so that they have a chance to put things right before your visit is spoilt. The AA does not undertake to arbitrate between you and the establishment, or to obtain compensation or engage in correspondence.

Date:

Your name (block capitals)

Your address (block capitals)

....

....

....

.... e-mail address:

Comments (please include the name & address of the establishment)

....

....

....

....

....

....

(please attach a separate sheet if necessary)

We may use information we hold about you to write, e-mail or telephone you about other products and services offered by us and our carefully selected partners. Information may be disclosed to other companies in the Centrica group (including those using the British Gas, Scottish Gas, One-Tel and AA brands) but we can assure you that we will not disclose it to third parties.

Please tick here if you DO NOT wish to receive details of other products or services from the AA.

PTO

Have you bought any other AA Britain's Best guides or other accommodation, restaurant, pub, or food guides recently? If yes, which ones?

....

....

Why did you buy the guide? To find a place for tea..

For a celebration   On holiday   While shopping

Break while travelling

other...

How often do you visit a place for tea? (circle one choice)

more than once a month   once a month   once in 2-3 months

once in six months   once a year   less than once a year

Please answer these questions to help us make improvements to the guide:

Which of these factors are most important when choosing a place for tea?

Price   Location   Awards/ratings   Service

Decor/surroundings   Previous experience
Recommendation

Other (please state):...

Do you read the editorial features in the guide?.....................................

Do you use the location atlas?...

Which elements of the guide do you find the most useful when choosing somewhere to have tea?

Description   Photo   Rating

Can you suggest any improvements to the guide?

....

....

....

....

Please send this form to:
AA
Lifestyle Guides,
The Automobile Association,
Fanum House,
Basingstoke RG21 4EA

Readers' Report form

or fax: 01256 491647
or e-mail: lifestyleguides@theAA.com

If you've enjoyed Afternoon Tea at a teashop, tea room or in a hotel not recommended in this guide, why not tell us about it?

Please note, however, that if you have a complaint to make during a visit, we strongly recommend that you discuss the matter with the establishment management there and then so that they have a chance to put things right before your visit is spoilt. The AA does not undertake to arbitrate between you and the establishment, or to obtain compensation or engage in correspondence.

Date:

Your name (block capitals)

Your address (block capitals)

....

....

....

.... e-mail address:

Comments (please include the name & address of the establishment)

....

....

....

....

....

....

(please attach a separate sheet if necessary)

We may use information we hold about you to write, e-mail or telephone you about other products and services offered by us and our carefully selected partners. Information may be disclosed to other companies in the Centrica group (including those using the British Gas, Scottish Gas, One-Tel and AA brands) but we can assure you that we will not disclose it to third parties.

Please tick here if you DO NOT wish to receive details of other products or services from the AA.

PTO

Have you bought any other AA Britain's Best guides or other accommodation, restaurant, pub, or food guides recently? If yes, which ones?

....

....

Why did you buy the guide? To find a place for tea..

For a celebration   On holiday   While shopping

Break while travelling

other...

How often do you visit a place for tea? (circle one choice)

more than once a month   once a month   once in 2-3 months

once in six months   once a year   less than once a year

Please answer these questions to help us make improvements to the guide:

Which of these factors are most important when choosing a place for tea?

Price   Location   Awards/ratings   Service

Decor/surroundings   Previous experience
Recommendation

Other (please state):...

Do you read the editorial features in the guide?.......................................

Do you use the location atlas?...

Which elements of the guide do you find the most useful when choosing somewhere to have tea?

Description   Photo   Rating

Can you suggest any improvements to the guide?

....

....

....

....

How can I get away without the hassle of finding a place to stay?

Booking a place to stay can be a time-consuming process. You choose a place you like, only to find it's fully booked. That means going back to the drawing board again. Why not ask us to find the place that best suits your needs? No fuss, no worries and no booking fee.

Whatever your preference, we have the place for you. From a rustic farm cottage to a smart city centre hotel - we have them all. Choose from around 8,000 quality rated hotels and B&Bs in Great Britain and Ireland.

Just **AA** sk.

Hotel Booking Service
www.theAA.com

You may contact us using a Textphone on 0870 243 2456.
Information is available in large print, audio and Braille on request

Notes